THE VERY WORST OF CONFESSIONS

Books by the same author
available from HarperCollins

CONFESSIONS
FURTHER CONFESSIONS
ON THIS DAY IN HISTORY

with Martin Wroe
SNOGGING
THE BIG MATCH

THE VERY WORST OF CONFESSIONS

More appalling misdeeds from the Radio 1 FM Breakfast Show

SIMON MAYO

Illustrated by Matt

Marshall Pickering
An Imprint of HarperCollins*Publishers*

Marshall Pickering is an Imprint of
HarperCollins*Religious*,
Part of HarperCollins*Publishers*,
77–85 Fulham Palace Road, London W6 8JB

First published in Great Britain
in 1993 by Marshall Pickering

1 3 5 7 9 10 8 6 4 2

A catalogue record for this book is
available from the British Library

ISBN 0 551 02806 8

Printed and bound in Great Britain by
HarperCollinsManufacturing Glasgow

CONTENTS

INTRODUCTION

Here we go again . . .

Welcome to volume three of the nation's favourite petty crime compendium. If *Crimewatch* ever put a book out, they would be hard pushed to come up with an assortment of sins as scandalous as this. On top of that, they would never get the actors to take part in the re-enactments. I mean, who in their right minds would lie in a morgue next to a whole row of dead bodies (what *is* the collective noun for stiffs?), have '43 Commando Royal Marines' tattooed across their chest, or perform horrible acts with hamsters, falcons and assorted cows?

If any police station is interested in obtaining the names and addresses to go with the confessions, please get in touch. But be warned, I have an extensive file marked 'Uncorroborated Police Confessions', and I think the Director of Public Prosecutions would be interested. Not that the DPP file is exactly empty!

As ever, thanks to my forgiveness collective of Rod, Dianne, Ric and various studio managers. And to you of course, for laughing so much you were prepared to fork out a fiver for this book!

For my son Ben
on the understanding he never
does anything as naughty
as the contributors to this
book

1

The Caring Professions?

Estate agents, footballers, politicians, lawyers, mafia hit-men,
bouncers, second-hand car salesmen, record company
promotions staff and off-shore bankers . . . to receive
confessions from any of them would raise no eyebrows,
elicit no gasps of surprise. We assume they're all crooks
anyway. But when you start getting stories from the
supposedly trustworthy sections of mankind, you know it's
only a matter of time before the whole fabric of society
crumbles. (That's enough of the Lord Tebbit routine for
now. Ed.)

Dear Simon,

I have a confession to make that regards the time when I was a surgical registrar in the northern parts of the country. I had an operating list to do one morning, and one of the patients was a young man who was for treatment to an ingrowing toenail: a very unpleasant condition. I examined him before the list and saw that the offending appendage was truly revolting, with the edges of his toenail turning green and brown due to the infected tissue. As another doctor had seen him in the clinic, I looked in his case notes to see what my boss had said. There are several different operations that can be done for an ingrowing toenail, and my boss's handwriting was not very legible. I thought that he had written 'radical excision of his toenail' which means removing the nail and the tissue that the nail grows from, so that the nail will not grow back, thus giving a permanent cure. I therefore shoved a large probe under his nail, grabbed it with a large pair of forceps, and tugged it off with an almighty pull, which would have made Herr Flick of the Gestapo proud. I then showed the nail to the watching student nurses, one of whom promptly fainted in a heap in the corner. I finished the operation very neatly, bandaged his toe, and went into the office to write the notes. I then realized that what my boss had written was 'a lateral excision of his toenail', which means trimming the side of the nail, leaving it still in place but narrower than normal. I later explained to the patient that I had done a different operation than planned as I thought that it would give him a better chance of a permanent cure (the latter part of which is true), however the whole truth was that I couldn't read my boss's writing.

Can I be forgiven for giving my patient a toe that looked like half a squashed sausage? It's not a mistake that I'll ever make again as I am now in brain surgery and no longer have dealings with feet.

Best Wishes,
Frank.

Dear Father Simon, Sister Dianne and Brother Rod,

A few years ago I was working as a senior radiographer in a huge teaching hospital which was about to open its new 'Imaging Modality' – ie an MRI body scanner. (MRI = Magnetic Resonance Imaging) – which, instead of using X-Radiation to make an image, uses a very strong magnetic field and radio frequency waves.

Before this new bit of 'kit' could be opened up and used on the public, it had, of course, to undergo an awful lot of tests which were under the supervision of various engineers from the manufacturers, several physicists, and a Professor of Radiology. This happy chappy put it about that he was a real workaholic and expected everyone else to be the same. Of course, my colleague (let's call him Jim) and I who'd been seconded to work with this team, being dedicated health service professionals, were of the same opinion! Most of the time. But not on Christmas Eve!

Anyway – it was Christmas Eve and traditionally the Imaging Department (ie X-Ray) had a lunchtime bash (no alcohol of course) with lots of scrummy food which we didn't get from the canteen! Jim and I had been looking forward to getting off at lunchtime to dive into the goodies when – lo and behold – the evil Prof. appeared with an idea for yet another test we could set up for him!

'But it's the Christmas "do" today!' we shouted in unison.

'So what?' said Scrooge. 'Come on, chaps, if you get on with it you'll be done by about half past four!'

With this he spun on his heel and was gone, a golf bag slung nonchalantly over his arm.

Muttering to ourselves, and to anyone else who would listen, we hatched our plan. We decided that one of us would stay put and begin to set up the test, while the other went over to the 'do' to bring back some goodies for the rest of the long afternoon. So, muggins set to at the scanner while Jim (who had bigger pockets) went off for the grub.

On his return, he had an evil gleam in his eye. He produced various bits and pieces for us to eat, along with a couple of paper hats, and we started nibbling.

'I met the Prof. on my way, you know,' said Jim, 'and he said he'd drop in about four o'clock to see how it was going.'

'Great. That means he'll probably think of something else for us to do and we'll be here all Christmas Day too,' I moaned.

'Not if we think of something for him to do first,' gloated Jim, who obviously had had an idea.

So it was that about 3.55 that afternoon I was rushing back from the nearest ward kitchen with four very hot mince pies, straight from the microwave oven. At 4.00 on the dot they were sitting neatly on a napkin in the body of the scanner, steaming gently. At about 4.05, in walked the Prof.

'Just in time', I said. 'Would you like a mince pie?'

The golf must have gone well, as he smiled (though it could have been wind) and said he would.

'Here we are,' said Jim, reaching inside the scanner. 'Nice and hot. How long was that?'

'Oooh,' I said, looking at my watch, 'About two minutes, I think.'

'Right. We'll have to remember that,' said Jim, just managing to keep a straight face.

Jim handed a pie to the Prof., who looked at it in disbelief.

'It's hot,' he stammered. 'How come it's hot?'

We said nothing, just looked pointedly at the shiny new scanner.

'That's not supposed to happen!' Prof. shouted, hands over his balding pate.

'There's something seriously wrong here,' he said as he sank into a chair. 'I'd better check some figures.'

By 4.30, sure enough, Jim and I had finished our little task, but the Prof. was still there in his office, poring over computer printouts and scribbling down equations. Goodness knows how long he was there, we didn't wait to find out.

I'd better add at this point that *NO body scanners, whether conventional X-Ray or MRI, cause ANY FORM OF HEATING TO THE BODY INSIDE IT*. We would have thought that a boffin like Prof. would have realized the joke pretty soon. We put it down to stress caused by it being Christmas Eve and him without a prezzy for Mrs Prof.

So, I ask forgiveness on behalf of Jim and myself for frightening the poor man out of his wits and for the long, cold night he spent working out where all the heat had come from. I also ask forgiveness for the wonderful present Mrs Prof. didn't get until the January sales.

Jackie.

Dear Simon & the Breakfast Crew,
This confession (which is only one of many!) goes back to 1983 and is
really a family confession.

My husband is a funeral director, and the family were living in a flat
above the offices and chapels of rest.

Our children were young and totally unconcerned about the
inhabitants who were laid to rest in the chapel below their bedroom!
Our middle daughter was only two years old and was one of those
children who never needed any sleep at night. Every night she would
get up, wanting to play – unfortunately the rest of us didn't!

So, she would wander around the flat chattering away to her dolls,
teddies and stuffed toys instead.

However, one night she never appeared and we thought 'Hooray!
she's slept all night.' Really pleased at getting a full night's sleep, my
husband got up and went downstairs to work.

Later that day a little old lady arrived at the office to see her dear
departed prior to his funeral. Normal practice is for the funeral
director to check on the body first, but being pushed for time, my
husband escorted the old lady straight into the chapel of rest.

When they opened the door, it was evident where our daughter
had been during the night. The coffin was lying in all its majesty –

surrounded by 27 stuffed toys, teddies and dolls (including the dolls pram!). Sarah had obviously found a new playmate during the night, one that could not tell her to shut up and go back to bed!!

We ask forgiveness from the old lady, and also from the dear departed, who had obviously been subjected to a night of the most boring, childish, gibberish imaginable, on what should have been a peaceful night before being laid to rest.

Yours hopefully,
The Family.

Dear Father Simon, Sister Dianne and the Most Reverend Rod,
Having heard your request for confessions from funeral directors recently, I could remain silent no longer. I am not a funeral director but my mother and father both have businesses so I feel I am qualified to contribute to your confessions spot. Spending the tender years of my childhood with two funeral directors has given me a more practical view on death, a subject which is usually considered to be too morbid to talk about by people in general. The business of seeing people off to that better place is a normal subject of discussion in our family. In the early days of my mother's business, my brother and I were taken to primary school in the hearse as this doubled up as the family saloon. Rather than think this odd, my friends thoroughly enjoyed trips in this spacious vehicle, taking turns to lie down in the back.

Anyway, the purpose of this letter is to confess an unfortunate misdemeanour carried out by my dad and to seek full absolution for him on his behalf.

A few years ago, following a very tasteful service at the local crem, the ashes of a client were picked up by my dad in the normal fashion. These were then placed carefully in an ashes casket ready to be buried. The family of the deceased requested that the ashes be interred by their local vicar in the churchyard near to their home. The ashes interment was arranged by my father with the vicar, whose availability was somewhat limited due to numerous weddings, christening and church services to be conducted. The only free day being the next Saturday. After confirming the arrangements with the family, all that my dad needed to do was deliver the casket to the vicar. That Friday afternoon, he asked one of his assistants to take it to the vicarage. The ashes were placed in a cardboard box together with the vicar's fee. When arriving at the house, the assistant placed the box in the garage as previously instructed by the vicar, who was taking a service that afternoon and would not be there. An hour later, there was a phone call from the vicar asking my dad when he could expect to receive the ashes. Somewhat puzzled, my dad told him that they had been brought down already but he would check with his assistant. The assistant explained that the ashes had been placed in the garage as instructed. My dad informed the vicar of this. Ten minutes later, the vicar was on the phone again. He had searched the garage and could not find the ashes. Beginning to sound harassed, dad sent the assistant back to the vicarage so he could show him exactly where he had put the casket.

The assistant met the vicar outside the garage. On entering, the assistant pointed in disbelief to where he had placed the box containing the ashes. There was now just an empty space and all the boxes and other items resembling junk which had been there had also disappeared. It was then that the horrifying realization of what had happened dawned on the vicar. About the same time as the assistant had delivered the casket, the local Scouts had arranged to empty the contents of the vicar's garage and take the items to their fund-raising jumble sale which was being held on Saturday. The Scouts had obviously taken the box containing the ashes casket with the other boxes and sundry items.

The vicar and my dad's assistant went immediately to the village hall where the jumble sale was to take place. To add insult to injury, the lights in the hall were not working. The assistant had to search endless rows of boxes, bags, bin liners and cases full of jumble in the dark with the help of an ancient pocket torch which he had borrowed from one of the bemused Cub Scouts. After two hours of backbreaking searching, the assistant managed to find the prayer mat which was to be used by the vicar during the service, so he knew he was getting warm. Finally, three hours later, the ashes casket appeared, to the relief of everyone present.

I wish to seek absolution for my dad from all of you so his soul may rest in peace when his time for departing this earth takes place. I also wish to seek forgiveness from the Scouts who were subjected to a verbal battering from the irate assistant for taking the ashes by mistake and finally from the spirit of the deceased whose bodily remains nearly ended up on the tombola. I know that my dad will not be listening to this as he listens to Radio 4, but please don't hold this against him when considering this plea for forgiveness.

Clare.

Dear Simon et al,

Our story takes place in 1986 when I was supervising an old folks day centre in the Keresley area of Coventry. Immanuel Christian Centre was a haven for around twenty elderly and infirm locals and provided them with lunch and activities for five days a week. By some strange coincidence my wife Helena also worked at the day centre as a care assistant (this has nothing at all to do with nepotism as I'm sure you will understand).

Picture the scene on Tuesday lunchtime as Helena welcomed these lovely old biddies to the centre. She took their coats, showed them to their seats and made them feel at home. One old soul, however, lingered behind by the entrance obviously wanting to discuss some personal matter with Helena. Mrs B was a bright, intelligent seventy-five-year-old but unfortunately her sight was beginning to fail.

'Helena, my dear,' began Mrs B, in an embarrassed way, 'could you help me? I've been using this tube of Super Denture Fixative Cream for a few days but it doesn't seem to work very well and it tastes awfully of rotten fish. Could you read the small printed address on the tube for me and write it down in large letters so I can contact the manufacturers and complain?'

Helena took the tube but she didn't need to read the small print. Written across the product in large letters were the words PREPARATION-H. Yes the old biddy had been massaging pile ointment into her gums for the last two weeks in the forlorn hope that it would stop the embarrassment of her false teeth jumping around uncontrollably. Instead she suffered the embarrassment of rotten-fish-halitosis.

Our confession, Simon, is not that we smiled or giggled but that we laughed until our sides hurt, all at the expense of this poor soul who had been a pillar of society for so many years. And that we repeated the story, not once, but many times, adding embellishments such as: 'It makes you wonder what she used to treat the haemorrhoids.' and 'I bet she had the widest smile in Coventry.'

Only now do we seek forgiveness from you because, unfortunately,

Mrs B has left this world for a far better place and so we cannot ask her face to face.

Please forgive us for we have sinned, we should never have laughed at this older and more mature lady, even if she did stick denture fixative up her bum.

Yours hopefully,
Mark.

2

Doing Unto Others . . .

The Spanish Inquisition, the Crusades, holy wars, fatwahs – the
religious world has had a lot to confess over the centuries. Here
we continue that great tradition. They may not all be confessions
on the scale of the Bishop of Galway's, but they are none the less
immensely significant. They prove that those of a holy
disposition are . . . are . . . well, exactly the
same as everyone else.

Dear Father Mayo, Sister Dianne, and most reverent Breakfast Crew,
This story goes way back into the mists of time (about 15 years ago)
when I was an altar boy.

I had my name down to do a requiem along with two other altar
servers – whom we will call Al and Tim. As per the rules, we arrived
about half an hour before the mass was about to start and as we were
getting ready, Al remarked on a strong pungent odour that was
hanging around in the air.

After a lot of searching, we discovered that the smell was originating
from the head of Tim. After discussing what we should do, Al and
myself did the good and honest thing and beat Tim up so he would tell
us what the heinous aroma was. It turned out that the smell was from
some nasty substance used to kill head lice that he had to wash his hair
with twice a day.

Anyway, Al and I were to be acolytes (the guys who had to carry the
candles) and Tim was the thurible bearer (the one who waves the
incense burner). The hearse arrived outside the church, so we
arranged ourselves in the correct order for the funeral procession.
Tim with the thurible at the front. Al and I with the candles and the
priest behind us. Now all we had to wait for was the coffin to be carried
out of the hearse, and we would make our way down the aisle to
escort the coffin and mourners into the church.

The pall bearers seemed to have some trouble, so we were waiting
quite a while for the procession to start. As the candle holders were
very heavy, the best way to hold them for any amount of time was to
rest the base against your hip and hold the candle out about 45° in
front of you, so that's what Al and I did. After about four minutes, the
pall bearers seemed to get their act together and started moving. Al
turned to tell the priest what was happening and we heard a hissing,
popping, crackling noise then an instant later a loud woof sound. After
turning to see what the noise was we noticed that Al's candle had
touched Tim's hair. Not only was the concoction on the hair supposed
to kill lice, but seemingly it was also very flammable indeed.

The show must go on, so we started down the aisle with the acolytes

23

laughing so much that they were crying, the thurible bearer's head smoking more than the incense, and a very displeased priest trying his best to read out the text of the mass.

Needless to say, the team of Al, Tim and myself were never asked to serve a requiem again.

I do not seek forgiveness for annoying the priest with our sniggering throughout the mass, but I wish to be forgiven for the way in which we walked towards the mourners with Tim looking like something out of a Tom and Jerry cartoon with Al and I laughing behind him, thus upsetting the poor family even more than they were already.

Thinking back, Al should have patented his method of ridding head infestations. Tim's problem never did return. Neither did his hair – properly!

Yours seeking forgiveness,
Chris.

Dear Simon Mayo,

I had been visiting my family in South Wales. Being a religious type, I was attending the evening service in the local Baptist church, on the final Sunday of my visit. The service had been a particularly moving one, incorporating a baptism by total immersion, the way they do in Baptist churches . . .

After the service, everyone was invited to stay for a cup of tea in the large room at the back of the church. I decided not to accept this kind invitation, having previously sampled the delights of Baptist church tea.

So I said goodbye to various people I knew and was on the point of leaving when I realized I hadn't said goodbye to one particular friend. Enquiring her whereabouts, I was informed that she was 'out the back making the tea'. I was somewhat unfamiliar with the layout of the church, but eventually found my way to a room where a large number of the congregation had gathered to brave the tea, and chat. The corner of this room was curtained off. Remembering that I'd seen a large water urn behind the curtain earlier on in the day, I assumed (incorrectly) that my friend was behind it making the tea. So with a great shriek of 'What are you doing behind that curtain?!!', I flung it back with a melodramatic flourish . . . to reveal the pastor and his helpers, stripped to their underwear, changing out of their wet clothes. It's hard for me to say who was the most embarrassed – me or them. We all froze – unfortunately for them, I froze with the curtain still held open. Behind me, the room fell silent as the rest of the congregation enjoyed this unexpected treat. It was like a video freeze frame. The pastor remained poised on one leg, with the other leg half in, half out of his trousers. His assistants stood motionless in a similar state of undress . . .

After what seemed an eternity I recovered sufficiently to drop the curtain. Gradually the buzz of conversation resumed as I beat a hasty retreat.

I never did say goodbye to my friend. Somehow, it no longer seemed important. Besides who knows what I might have found had I continued to hunt around the church.

Soo.

Dear Father Mayo,

It all began back in 1979/80 when I was in Bible college in Manchester. Living in a hostel with the other students, we had to study very late at night and wake up very early in the morning for lectures.

I was in my second year when we welcomed a student from another part of the world, who was a very devout and enthusiastic believer. Without quoting every verse in the Bible to counteract everything one said and did, he would always look for an opportunity to grab you by the scruff of your neck and breathe the fear of God in you. As students we needed to keep up the college requirements which meant studying very hard for exams and handing in assignments on time, and we needed all the sleep we could get – every extra minute of sleep was very welcome, cutting it very fine to reach lectures in time (8 am).

The crunch came when our devout friend would wake up in the early hours of the morning (4 am) and pray at the top of his voice. My room being directly above his I would get the full force of his decibels. Then, one by one, the other blokes would wake up moaning, but never did anything. I said to myself, 'I've got to put a stop to this.'

In those days I used to have an electric guitar with an amplifier with an echo effect. So the plot was hatched. By listening to my friend below I knew exactly what he would say, so I wrote down what I was going to say in reply.

At 4 am the next morning he started with his confessions and requests to Him in the Heavens above. I began to put my plan into action – the amplifier was switched on and the echo mode was effected. I replied to his questions and requests by saying 'Yes, my son'; 'I bless you my son'; 'Keep up the good work'; etc etc. Then in a louder voice I said, 'In the future when you pray I would like you to do so very quietly and keep your voice down, after all I am not deaf, and I can hear your very slightest whisper. Think of your other brothers who are resting. If you want to shout why not go to Switzerland and shout at the mountains – you can shout at the top of your voice, and there your work will be appreciated?' To this came the reply from my friend, 'If it's Your will then I will obey'.

By this time my ear was glued to the floor, since his voice had dropped to a mere semi shout. I had to contain myself from screaming with laughter by burying my face in a pillow. The other people in the hostel began to stir so I shut everything down and acted innocently, wanting to know what was going on.

It did not stop there – there's more – every Wednesday everyone in the college had to attend chapel. My dear friend got up in chapel to share his experience of the previous night, saying that God had spoken to him and he was terminating his training and going to Switzerland to share his experience. Everyone was amazed but shook his hand and congratulated him. I could not face him so I took my exit hastily. Within a few weeks he left for Switzerland and I did not have the guts to wish him well, and say goodbye.

To this day I have not heard of him. So wherever you are, brother Jacob, I ask your forgiveness. I also ask forgiveness from the staff and students of the college for the trick I played, but all I wanted was an extra precious moment of sleep for everyone else. I went on to graduate and now have a very responsible job (but not in the Church – I have since left my calling).

Siri.

AND BRING ME A CUP OF TEA...

Father Mayo,

About four years ago I used to be an altar server at my local church, St Wilfred's. St Wilfred's being a small Catholic church meant that it was not always full, but the same old people were there every week. It was early one Sunday when I committed the deadly sin. The Church used to have two masses. One at nine thirty and one at eleven, and I used to serve in them both, along with a friend. The priest was always boring and always very strict. My friend and I decided to liven up the mass by substituting the water for gin that I had taken from home.

As you might have guessed the priest said mass at nine thirty and drank the gin, he said mass again at eleven and drank the gin. His words were already beginning to sound slurred and his eye and hand co-ordination was not working, as he managed to burn his hand in the candles on the altar.

When mass was over a member of the congregation came over to my friend and me, and asked us if we thought the priest was drunk. I don't know what came over us but we said yes, he was drinking before mass and was over the pub before he came here. We had to go and get him out.

Well it didn't take long for the word to get around that the priest was drunk when he said mass.

I ask for forgiveness for spiking his drink, telling lies about him and causing the priest much embarrassment and stress.

Yours hoping to be forgiven,
J.

Dear Father Simon,

I was not even a twinkle in my mother's eye when both my parents went to Tanzania as medical missionaries after finishing medical school. However the twinkle appeared and – not much later – so did I.

Our little village of Mvumi (which means 'wind' by the way) was indeed little, and so it was with great excitement that the local church welcomed our bishop one Sunday, who arrived in a sophisticated 4-wheel drive Land-Rover about the time that I was three and my chum, Christopher Keith, about four.

You must understand, Kind Father, that in Tanzania it is very hot. Even when it is cold it is hot, and the day that the bishop came was a scorcher. It was on days like this that Chris and I had found that when we were fortunate enough to come across such a rare and luxurious item as a bicycle – or even a motorbike – we could send a soothing breeze across our sweating brows by pressing a certain point on the tyres.

Imagine our delight when, that scorching hot Sunday morning, we found in our own village a vehicle with four huge tyres – each packed with refreshing, cool air. We eagerly set to work easing our discomfort, and it was with great disappointment that we drained the last hiss of air and had to leave.

I beg the forgiveness of Bishop Madinda who returned to find his vehicle four inches lower than he had left it, and of whoever had to work in the African heat pumping up the tyres with a foot pump. I also ask that my sins be forgotten by my parents, who had to face such an early rebellion against the church, and by Chris on whom I grassed and whose parents were a lot more angry than mine were with me.

Yours coolly,
Matthew.

Dear Father Simon,

Forgive me as I have sinned. It was twenty years ago when I was chorister and our parish church had a coffee morning and jumble sale to raise funds for one of the church appendages . . . the spire.

The coffee morning was a roaring success, and raised the princely sum of eleven quid. However there were several items left unsold one of which was a tailor's dummy. The problem was what to do with it and the other items left over. Eventually they were all bundled into a storeroom along with the broken chairs and ping pong tables that most churches seem to collect.

It was whilst in the storeroom that my fellow conspiritors and I hatched our plan. With someone keeping lookout the dummy's arms were detached just above the elbow as I remember. Then it was off to the graveyard.

Once again lookouts were posted and a suitable grave found. The arms were then planted just down from the headstone, we all retired to the bushes to await results. I would like to apologise to the old lady who tended the graves, and the guests of a wedding who had started to arrive. As their cries of horror reached us we scarpered.

The happy couple attending the wedding probably wondered why the trebles collapsed with laughter when the vicar said 'they should join their hands together in holy matrimony'.

Still it was all harmless fun really.

Yours faithfully,
Jamie.

Dear Simon,

I am now a Youth Pastor, I am also the son of a Baptist minister and have always lived in a manse. The following happened eight years ago, whilst I was still living at home.

I had just returned back from ten months in America and like most eighteen-year-olds I had picked up a number of things from my American friends. We had a habit of answering the phone with peculiar messages. Answering machines weren't as common then and this meant we had the added advantage of hearing the caller's startled response.

One Saturday morning we were all in the kitchen, my mum, dad and sister, when the telephone rang. I threatened to answer the phone in my own inevitable way, not knowing who was on the other end. My family half-heartedly told me not to, so I proceeded anyway, with:

'Hi, this is Malc's Morgue, you stab 'em, we'll slab 'em, 24-hour stiff service.'

My family burst out laughing as they realized what I said; however, the person on the other end of the line wasn't making quite so much noise. Eventually the person ringing told me who they were and asked to speak to my father. After a great struggle he managed to control his laughter and speak intelligibly down the phone.

It turned out to be someone from his previous church in London, to inform him of the death of one of the church members and to ask him to take the funeral. Fortunately for me the person ringing was a good friend of my parents and although at the time they were quite shocked they took it very well in the end.

I have to admit that now I stick to funny messages only when I have dialled the phone number and know who is likely to answer it. My wife and I are expecting a child in November and I can assure you they will grow up knowing better than to make the same mistake as me.

Yours sincerely,
Malcolm.

Dear Father Simon,

For almost fifteen years I have been the organist in a large parish church in Cardiff. However, about a year ago, my position was in grave jeopardy. A new vicar was introduced to the parish, but the two of us did not get on at all.

Therefore, it came as no surprise when he announced in the parish newsletter that I was to get an assistant. This would be to 'help lighten my burden'(!) I was of course outraged; I made a tidy packet out of this job – not from the normal services of course, but from weddings and the like.

One Sunday morning in January after the Eucharist, I was introduced to 'George', my new 'workmate'. The following Sunday, George sat behind me in the organ loft and tut-tutted his way through the service as I played. I had decided to finish with Widor's 'Toccata' but I no longer felt confident enough. Instead I ended the service with Bach's Air in G.

A week later was George's first service which went without a hitch. He finished with Widor's 'Toccata' and played it perfectly. According to the new timetable, George was due to play the following Sunday as well – I knew I had a week to act. I got hold of a copy of the weekly hymn sheet and produced a very credible copy with some minor alterations, changing the hymn numbers so that George would play the wrong tunes!!

The first hymn was that old favourite 'Love Divine' but from the organ loft came 'When I survey the wondrous cross'. The look on the faces of the congregation was of complete confusion. George meanwhile was completely carried away, playing his heart out – not noticing that anything was wrong. However, after the communion hymn even he knew something was up. While he was taking communion, I swapped the hymn sheets back and the final hymn was the correct one.

George tried to protest his innocence after the service, but the vicar would have none of it. He told George that he could play at a wedding on Saturday – it was his last chance!

Before the wedding service at 2 pm, I took George down the pub and told him not to worry and that the vicar was quite senile. However as soon as the ceremony began, George was doomed! He played the wrong organ voluntary, the wrong first hymn and an incorrect chant for the psalm. Not only that, but a few of the stops on the organ were 'out of order'...

Needless to say, George was not paid by the bride's father (an influential member of the parish) because his daughter was so upset. The vicar and the father confronted George afterwards and noticed the smell of beer on his breath – No one has seen George since...

Simon, I'd like to apologize to George – it wasn't really his fault after all. I'd like to apologize to the vicar for ruining his relationship with a member of his parish, but most of all I'd like to apologize to the bride and groom for ruining their happy day. Simon, if you forgive me and read this letter out, I promise that I'll play an arrangement of Albinonis' Confession Music for Strings in G minor in church on Sunday.

Will you, brother Rod or bride-to-be Dianne forgive me?

Yours sincerely,
Morgan the Organ...

Dear Holy Father,

I too am a holy father and back in the early 80s I was priest-in-charge of a parish in rural Derbyshire. I enjoyed my time there very much. Lovely people, beautiful scenery and though my parishioners were not the most devout in the land, we had a good attendance record and we were on the up generally speaking. Being a Londoner by birth I had been a little bit worried as to how well I would be accepted, but after a few months I had clearly passed the test and notwithstanding regular 'southern softie' type references, I was as you would say 'one of the lads'.

So along came Christmas Eve 1985. Now it's true some people think we only work at Christmas and on Sundays – a gross travesty – but this festive season things had been particularly trying. On top of the usual trips to schools, old folks' homes, non-stop carol service planning and pastoral calls, we had just had seven funerals in three weeks *and* most unusually for the time of year two weddings. You can imagine Christmas Eve found me slightly more stressed out than usual. We had two services on Christmas Eve, a 7.30 pm family communion and a midnight mass. Having had a successful 7.30 – good singing and a splendid atmosphere – I had – as priests do – to finish the consecrated wine. In this case the two goblets were both half full.

As I was setting up for the midnight service, a couple who had quite recently arrived in the parish popped in to see if I would care to enjoy a seasonal glass of good cheer at the local. Working out I probably had about two hours before I should be back, I said that I would be delighted. The trouble with being a priest in a pub at Christmas is that everyone (and I do mean everyone) wants to buy you a drink. I let most of them. As I said it had been a difficult few days and I thought what the heck – I'm not driving and I know the service well enough to get by.

The problem was that I had learnt my drinking with Watney's Red Barrel and I had never heard of Theakstons' Old Peculier. I did that night and my parishioners knew I did. Father Simon, I would like forgiveness for the following:

Announcing to the congregation that the first carol would be 'Father Christmas do not touch me'.

Belching twice in the service, once when my microphone was on.

Saying rather loudly to the organist, 'For heaven's sake, you old woman, can't you play any faster?'

and, worst of all, while shaking hands with the departing throng, greeting one married couple, the husband of whom I suspected to be having an affair with his secretary, with the words, 'Happy Christmas to you both. And your girlfriend.'

I know it was unforgivable, but perhaps you can help. I've since moved to Hampshire.

Peter.

Dear Father Mayo,
As funerals go, the service at the crematorium had been going quite
smoothly. The mourners looked suitably appreciative as I extolled the
virtues of the deceased and the strength of his faith. The final hymn,
before the committal, had a note of hopefulness about it in anticipation
of the body being sent on its way. Then came The Hitch.

After solemnly pronouncing the words 'We commit his body to be
cremated; ashes to ashes, dust to dust' I pressed the button to lower
the coffin to the furnaces – and nothing happened. It sat there,
immoveable on the podium. I pressed again, more firmly this time, but
still nothing happened. I looked anxiously at the faces of the relatives.
They were blank. Quickly I turned to another prayer. 'Bring comfort to
those in distress . . .' at the same time trying to hide my frantic efforts to
get the machinery moving. Another prayer followed. This time I
slammed my finger on the button so hard that great crackles of static
electricity burst from the speakers of the electronic organ. Even the
organist looked shocked.

At last, after yet another 'closing prayer' I decided to abandon all
further attempts to get the coffin to go down. I meandered past it to
the exit, moving in a mysterious way, still hopeful that the platform
might start to lower, but alas . . . I pulled the curtains closed by hand
and made a few mechanical sounding noises. The relatives filed out
looking embarrassed. They shook my hand limply. As far as I know, the
coffin may still be there. I need to be absolved of all further
responsibility for this body.

Yours sincerely,
Rob.

3

Duty Nobly Done

I regularly throw away the majority of the confessions I receive.
Not out of spite or laziness (well, not *primarily* out of spite or
or laziness) but because they are too unfunny/crude/involve
laxatives or are violently cruel. Into this last category come the
majority of military confessions. Not surprising I suppose. Here
though are five that slipped through my Maginot Line.

Dear Saintly Simon, Divine Dianne and Reverend Rod,

Having listened to 'Confessions' from Day I every morning on my way into work I feel the time has come to make my confession and seek your forgiveness.

I was a Lieutenant in the Women's Royal Naval Service until January 1992 and had always participated fully in any special or sporting activity regardless of any talent or aptitude required. It was with some pleasure therefore that I was picked for the team to represent my department in the annual Christmas 'It's a Knockout' competition (they were scraping the barrel by this stage).

The competition was always a fancy dress competition and our team always consisted of 90–100% girls. It was not surprising therefore that we were never able to win the first prize for sporting prowess due, mainly, to the Royal Marines ensuring that everything was twice as difficult by the time we got to it. However, remembering the motto 'It is not the winning that is important but the taking part', we entered every time. To make up for any inadequacies in the physical aspect of the competition we made sure that we would win the Fancy Dress competition and entered in more bizarre outfits each year.

Two years ago 'Batman – The Movie' was THE movie to see and we decided to go as Batman (all ten of us). We had one man, Dave, in the team and he decided to go as Batgirl despite the fact that he had a very healthy growth of beard and hairy legs. As the day of the competition approached the girls and Dave were busily making outfits and we hit on the idea of transporting ourselves from the workplace to the sports hall by Sherpa van cunningly disguised as a Batmobile.

The day of the competition dawned and at lunch time we all dressed up in black lycra leggings, black T Shirts with the Batman logo emblazoned on our chests, black plastic capes (thank goodness for bin bags) and black masks. We stuck black plastic wings to the side of the Sherpa van, a large Batman logo on the front and wired up speakers to the cassette player so that we could blast the whole naval establishment concerned with Batman music as we made our way up to the sports hall.

At 12.30 precisely we set off from the office to travel one mile up the hill to the sports hall with yours truly driving. We could only travel at about ten miles per hour as the wings were quite fragile. The music was blasting and we were all hanging out of the windows waving our capes at everybody and everything we passed. You will have guessed that we were determined to make an entrance.

As we drove up the main road of the naval base there were quite a large number of Ministry of Defence Police to be seen, far more than usual. We sang at them as we approached and waved the wings in their direction but the response was what you might call cool! We drove on assuming that the dinner in the police canteen must have been particularly bad that day. We turned onto the road which takes you up the steep hill to the sports hall and were confronted by a large number of senior ratings dressed in their best uniforms, medals and all, lining the streets. By this time I was beginning to suspect that there was something amiss and asked the members of the team if they knew what was happening. No one answered so I continued up the hill at a stately ten miles per hour, music blaring, lights flashing and ten 'Batmen' shrieking at the top of their voices.

We rounded the next corner to find yet more senior ratings and officers in their best uniforms, some of whom were just managing to suppress smiles. I again asked if anyone knew what was up and a little voice from the back said, 'Isn't it someone's funeral today?'

Realizing that the road we were on also took you to the church and the funeral cortege was only minutes, nay seconds, behind us I slammed my foot on the accelerator and screeched up the hill to the sports hall scattering well dressed officers by the wayside. We hid the 'Batmobile' behind some dustbins and sneaked into the competition hoping nobody would notice us which, in hindsight, was a bit naive since ten 'Batmen' could hardly sneak anywhere.

I would be eternally grateful if you could see your way to forgiving me for this grievous sin since it has haunted me since that day.

Yours grovellingly,
Alison.

Dear Simon,

My confession goes back a very very long time, when you were probably just a twinkle in your father's eye.

It all started when my husband and I were courting. We were both serving members of the Royal Air Force, dedicated to protecting this wonderful country from all enemies etc., etc. Each evening after a hard days protecting, we would all meet up in the Naafi (the erogenous zone of the station!) and enjoy a few gallons of rough cider.

One evening, closing time came and we staggered out into the cool summer's night. Well you know how it is Simon, we simply didn't want the evening to end there, we wanted to find a nice quiet place to discuss some serious issues, i.e. the weather, price of bread, etc., etc.

It was then that my husband, hatched his cunning plan. Well, I was quite shocked at his suggestion, and took a lot of persuading (all of 30 seconds). He explained that he had paid one of the cooks in the airmen's mess the extortionate fee of two pints, to leave one of the ground floor kitchen windows open when he locked up.

We met outside the open window and clambered in. The place was in complete darkness, as we made our way through the kitchen I could feel a strange crunching sound under my feet, but thought nothing of it.

At the end of the dining area, there was a lounge, with beautiful settees originating from the Rothschild mansion. They were filled with horsehair and wood shavings. We chose a particularly comfy one, and settled down to a couple of hours chatting! After our chat, my husband decided a cigarette would be nice, like you do, and being a little more sober by this time, we were conscious of the fact that the police patrolled around the camp at regular intervals, so we hid behind the settee to strike the light. As it lit, the match broke in two, the lit end shot forward in the direction of the settee!

The next thing I remember was a huge ball of flames engulfing first the settee then quickly spreading to the other furniture! Within seconds the whole place was on fire.

Well, we legged it! And as we retreated back through the kitchen, the flames lit up the kitchen floor, which was covered in cockroaches *with a look of shock and horror on their sweet little faces (dear little things, Dianne).*

We raced back to our respective blocks, and I just managed to get into bed before the entire camp was awakened by the sound of fire engines racing to tackle the blaze.

We have kept that secret for years for fear of being caught, but our conscience has now got the better of us. It certainly wasn't the thought that we might just get a mention on your show!

In conclusion, we would seek the forgiveness of the local fire brigade who, after a lengthy investigation decided the fire was caused by someone leaving a cigarette burning after the evening meal (eight hours earlier!) One last word in my defence, Dianne, none of the cockroaches suffered, they were clever enough to climb out the window behind us!

Yours faithfully,
Valerie.

Dear Simon,

I spent eight years in the Royal Marines, and it will come as no surprise to you when I say that the humour of the Forces in general can be rather harsh and cruel sometimes. It was only after leaving the Forces and attending teacher training college that I found that some of the things that had often had myself and fellow marines in stitches, failed to raise even a smile when told in civilian company. Gradually, as is always the case with us social beings, I learned to adapt and to relate different tales and to laugh at different things. But this one true story that I am about to tell you simply refused to die a death in my memory, and has haunted me for over 25 years.

I was awaiting the start of a specialist training course, and was given the job of unit postman, a job shared between two NCOs, and a role that always made whoever was doing it, very popular. People were always dropping in to our office to see if they had any mail, and Ben and I made everyone welcome, enjoying the chat and a laugh. Some people visited more often than others, and one young officer, who was a fresh faced 20-year-old, became a daily visitor, telling us about home, and his aspirations in the Marines. He was so keen and eager about his choice of career that his enthusiasm made us poke fun at him sometimes, for it was implicitly understood that we should not show too much enthusiasm for the Corps. Fate, as always, deals cruelly with those who have not learned the lesson about having a circumspect approach to the future, and our young officer appeared one day with a long and sorrowful face. It seemed that for medical reasons he was not to be allowed to continue his career, and he was to leave the Corps within a couple of months. Ben and I could have instantly named two dozen or more marines that were desperate to get out, yet here was fate decreeing that the keenest commando we'd ever met, should leave — how sad, how savage, how ironic.

It called for a night to remember, a night that our young friend could always look back on, to tell his children about one day, of how he painted Plymouth red in the company of two good mates who were sorry to see him go. So ashore we went, a few days before he was due to go home, and by 11 pm his eyes were glazed, and his legs no longer working. I won't bore you with the tawdry, bawdy details, but it was nothing new really, a poor man's 'Carry On . . .' script. However, the climax of the night which Ben and I had dreamed up, and which we'd been hysterical about in anticipation several times, finally arrived. In the small hours of the morning we sat him down in the tattoo parlour and as he looked down on his arm in a befuddled and puzzled way, the needle traced out in glorious Technicolor '43 Commando Royal Marines' with an upraised dagger central to the design. What a great night – a good few beers, and a story that we could tell and re-tell that would always raise a laugh.

Next morning Ben and I were on our rounds delivering the mail to the various offices, when we saw our young, very hung-over friend appear with two fellow officers, who were providing both physical and moral support for him. With no beating about the bush one of them approached us and said, 'That was a rotten thing to do last night.' I played the complete innocent. 'What do you mean?' 'I mean getting him tattooed,' he replied, somewhat belligerently. 'Oh, the tattoo,' I said. 'That's nothing to worry about, it's only a transfer, it will wash off.' Our young friend's face lightened, and his shoulders looked as though a great weight had been lifted from them. 'Will it?' he asked, scarcely able to believe his ears. 'No,' said Ben, and we fell about once more, delirious with the humour of the situation.

Many is the time I have thought about this over the years, and I have latterly truly and earnestly hoped that that tattoo did not cause him too much sorrow after he left the Corps. It has taken me a long time to sit down to expurgate the memory of the deed, but it was a great night out.

Taff.

Dear Father Mayo,

While working for the RAF as a Parachute Instructor at Abingdon, Oxfordshire, all new parachute course personnel were required to make two jumps from a balloon before jumping from an aircraft. The balloon resembled a barrage balloon from the Second World War with a fabricated steel basket slung below it. The basket would accommodate four would-be parachutists and the despatcher. The balloon is let up to a height of 1000 feet. This is controlled from the ground by a winch attached to it by a steel cable.

Once up there it is so quiet that you can literally hear a pin drop. The idea now is that each parachutist is called to the doorway, and stands with both hands grasping the sides of the basket. The despatcher gives two commands 'RED ON' and 'GREEN ON' to simulate the real thing, that is an exit from an aircraft.

Each member of the balloon is given a number, 1 to 4. I called No.1 to the door, and he stood there gripping the basket sides with his knuckles showing white and staring into space with large bulging eyes.

I gave him the 'RED ON' command and at this point he is supposed to take his right hand off the doorway and place it tightly over his chest on top of his reserve chute. This he duly did, on the 'GREEN ON' command he is supposed to release his other hand and fold it across his other arm and jump out.

What he actually did was to unfold his right arm and grab the basket with his right hand and fold his left arm across his chest. I shouted 'GREEN ON' again, and he repeated the sequence but vice versa. I politely told him to jump, but he refused. Oh dear I thought, he needs to be calmed down.

The floor of the basket has a removeable panel which slides back out of the way to reveal a large square hole. I chuckled to myself and slid the panel back. I put my hand on his shoulder and told him to calm down and step back away from the doorway. On this command I felt him relax and his eyes appeared to return to their sockets. He took two steps back and 'WHOOSH!' he was gone. His first jump under his belt, even though his exit was slightly unorthodox. His scream still echoes in my memory.

I then put the panel back in place, and called No. 2 to the doorway, surprisingly he went out without any hesitation, and so did Nos. 3 and 4. This did not happen on a regular basis as rumours and strange stories seem to spread quite rapidly.

I beg forgiveness from No. 1 as although it was a nice dry sunny say I am afraid that he had rather a 'SOGGY' landing.

Mike.

Dear Father Simon,

Forgive me, Father, for I have sinned. Almost two years ago, when I was in the RAF, we had to go for our medical. Going in alphabetical order I was near the end and had to listen to a string of complaints about ill-treatment, mainly embarrassment, at the hands of a ferocious Welsh female orderly. A little mischief would not go amiss, thought I. My turn came, the boys were not wrong, if Wales ever had a dragon this was her.

She thrust a bottle in my hand, pointed to a screen and barked her orders. I did my duty and duly handed back the bottle for her to test.

'There's something TERRIBLY wrong here,' she said, looking strangely from me to the bottle. I took the bottle from her and examined it. 'Looks all right to me!' I said and promptly swallowed the contents of said bottle. I should add at this point that I had filled the bottle with Castlemaine's finest lager when I was behind the screen and not the usual fluid you would expect.

I then called for assistance as the orderly had fainted. When quizzed as to what had happened I replied in all innocence that she had just keeled over and suggested as a parting shot that she may be in the family way, thus subjecting her to the ordeal we had all been through. I ask forgiveness from the orderly and your good selves.

Yours,
AC Wood, RAF.

4

. . . And Used in Evidence Against You

I often get a little nervous when I'm about to read a confession out on my wonderful show. This is usually because of fear: fear of revenge, legal action and imminent unemployment. When we had a 'police week' on the show recently I was careful not to go too far. Losing the willing support of the local constabulary was a price not worth paying. Be careful how loudly you laugh at this next selection.

Dear Father Simon,

It was in the winter of 1985, Father, in the city centre of Liverpool, that I was assigned the very responsible role of 'Tutor Constable' to the new recruit on our section. Due to the need to rely upon each other in a variety of circumstances we developed a very close working bond and, as part of his professional development, I encouraged my colleague to confide in me whenever he felt the need.

Thanks to the plethora of rather traumatic incidents to which he was exposed my colleague took me up on the invitation and regularly poured out his heart to me. I can honestly say, Father, that I fulfilled my role with dedication. However, my young recruit went one disclosure too far. He conveyed to me a very commonly held fear – it was the mind-numbing fear he had of dead bodies and his subsequent dread at the thought of dealing with one in the course of his duties.

Well, Father Simon, such an opportunity was too good to miss and as I possessed a sense of humour common to most police officers, i.e. warped and depraved, I shared this information with the rest of the section and we hatched a cunning plan.

The following week was to be the first that our young colleague, whom I will now refer to as Constable X, was to experience patrolling alone, a threshold in any officer's career and one that did not escape our attention.

Situated in a murky, dimly lit Victorian backstreet was the City Mortuary and it was to this ghoulish location that all of the bodies of people unfortunate enough to pass away during the night were taken and laid out. It was no coincidence that Constable X was posted to the beat that covered the said Mortuary and thus he assumed responsibility for the premises.

It was shortly after 5 am when the radio of Constable X crackled into life, breaking the silence of a cold, wintry night. From the radio room came the instruction to attend at the Mortuary and collect the wedding ring from the hand of Body No. 77 which had been laid out earlier that night by an officer from a neighbouring division who had forgotten to remove the ring when itemizing the deceased person's property.

It was a pale and drawn Constable X who walked into the station foyer a short time later to collect the key to the mortuary. As the station keeper passed him the key, lovingly adorned with a small wooden coffin as a key fob, he muttered some reassuring words about ignoring the reputation of the Mortuary as being the haunt of some notorious Liverpool ghosts. Constable X was not convinced and, putting on a brave face, ventured out into the cold night to discharge his unpleasant duty.

A biting wind was howling as Constable X approached the archway at the entrance to the mortuary, poorly lit by a solitary gas light. Nervously he placed the key in the lock and opened the door which, like that of all good mortuaries, was in grave need of a spot of oil. The design of the building was such that you had to walk the length of the main room in order to turn on the lights which, at 5 am and all alone, is something of a trial to those of a nervous disposition.

Constable X switched on his torch and started to walk along the tiled floor. The air was filled with the smell of formaldehide and several of the bodies were situated on trolleys in front of the refrigerators. Having reached the light switch he turned them on, took a deep breath and turned around. Initially he stood rooted to the spot before gathering himself and moving towards the nearest body that was lying on a trolley, covered by a white sheet.

Tentatively he checked the number on the small tag attached to the big toe of the body, protruding from beneath the sheet. Slowly he

moved along the bodies until he reached BODY 77. The left hand of the body could just be seen, adorned with the wedding ring that he sought. Even on such a cold night beads of sweat could be detected on the forehead of Constable X and his skin was pale and clammy. It was some time before he had composed himself enough to reach out for the cold, motionless hand. However, as he grasped hold of the said hand he let out a piercing scream and threw himself backwards onto the floor as the body suddenly sat up rigidly and exclaimed 'CAN I HELP YOU'. Constable X immediately assumed a state of absolute panic, screaming at the top of his voice and scampering backwards on the floor like a double-jointed crab.

Eventually he got back to his feet and sprinted towards the exit of the mortuary. However, his legs soon began to buckle again as, first to his right and then to his left, body after body began to sit up accompanied by much groaning. It was eventually on all fours that he disappeared into the night pursued only by the sound of raucous laughter.

Of course, the 'bodies' in question were in fact the warped work colleagues of Constable X, of whom I was one.

Constable X, traumatized beyond belief, sadly resigned the next day despite our reassurances that he had merely been subjected to an initiation ceremony.

Yours sinfully,
Ray.

Dear Simon,

During 1969 I was a serving police officer in the Metropolitan Police stationed at Tower Bridge 'nick'. I was young, in uniform and still a bit wet behind the ears, despite having been a member of the 'Force' for a whole year!

On this occasion I was on night duty, riding shotgun in the station van, my driver being a hefty lad called Rodney, who had a heart of gold. Before going any further it is necessary to explain that 'Nights' could be a bit boring, especially down around the Old Kent Road, so every chance we got to get involved in a 'call', we didn't hang around, we got stuck in.

On this particular night, at about 2 am, we answered a call to a serious disturbance at the Elephant and Castle. We, and about two hundred other units, who also were finding it quiet this night, attended and between us just about managed to deal with the three meths connoisseurs who could not agree who was having the cardboard box that night.

As we had not been called upon to get involved, we decided, as was the norm, to take the longest and most indirect route back to our station area, before continuing our patrol.

Imagine our delight when about half a mile into our 'expedition' we were accosted by a rather robust middle-aged lady who was obviously in distress. As tradition demanded we pulled over to see if we could be of assistance in her hour of need.

She explained that her husband had been to a local inn and having consumed more than his fair share, had left to go home early. When she arrived about an hour later, he was asleep on the settee and refused, or was unable, to get up to open the door.

The woman led Rodney and me to the house, and peering through the dusty window we could see 'hubby' sound asleep on the settee. We knocked and banged on the window and eventually managed to raise him, or at least his head. We explained the plight of his wife, but imagine our surprise when all we got was a string of abuse which even made poor Rodney blush!!

We explained to the woman that our hands, and not his neck, were tied, but she then burst into tears explaining that she had nowhere to go. Being the instant decision maker that I was, I persuaded Rodney to help the woman get in. With no windows open we decided that Rodney, because of his massive frame, should cave the door in. Easier said than done – on his first attempt he bounced back a good two feet. 'They don't make them like that any more,' he uttered. Unperturbed, and after a few more joint assaults, the door gave way. The woman could not thank us enough, and as we drove off into the dawn, she stood by the side of the road and waved her thanks.

Six am came and we went off to bed. Then all too soon came 10 pm, the next shift. As I walked into the station and before I could even wonder at the delights the coming night might hold, I was told by my sergeant to ring the Night Duty Inspector of the police station on whose area our heroic deed had occurred. I immediately phoned and was put through to the Inspector in question. He asked whether or not we had assisted a lady gain access to a house. My mind raced, I remembered the old police adage – admit nothing!! 'Of course not,' I told him, then asked with a rather frightened quiver in my voice, 'Why?'

'Because whoever it was, the stupid idiots helped her into her next door neighbour's house!!!'

Simon, the only person I seek forgiveness from is the person whose door we dented, but if that was the man who verbally abused us then – GOOD JOB!!!

Yours officially,
Peter.

Dearest Brethren and Sister,

My tale starts back in the upper sixth form at a secondary school not a big hit away from the Oval Cricket Ground in London.

In our year was what I can only describe as early primitive man. Ray was 6 ft tall, sexist, loud, brash, racist, homophobic etc., etc. Everything you'd hate in a man, Dianne. He and his cronies made life misery for the others in the sixth form, not to mention the rest of the school. Anyone who wasn't macho and didn't leer at his 'educational' magazines was a 'poofter' and God help you if you weren't a WASP. Luckily enough my best mate was 6 ft 4 and about as wide so some of us were left alone but we decided we'd had enough of his posturing, pouting and posing so we hatched a cunning plan. Cue Baldrick.

On his 18th birthday Ray decided to have a shandy or two in the local hostelry where most of the 6th form retired after school.

Unknown to Ray his cronies had clubbed together and got him a kissogram. So, at 6.30, after about 6 pints of lager, the kissogram arrived. Dressed very seductively in stockings, suspenders, short skirt, school tie and boater etc. as every schoolgirl looks of course. From our position at the other end of the bar we watched with morbid curiosity. The 'schoolgirl' took off some of Ray's clothing, but none of hers. The usual poem was read out and then the schoolgirl gave him a kiss. (It might be advisable for Dianne to shut her ears at this point.) A full bloodied tonsil tennis jobby. Then the 'schoolgirl' skipped off out of the door.

Ray couldn't believe it. His cronies couldn't believe it. Ray was full of it. He'd copped off with the kissogram girl. He was the boy. The Top Dog. Mr Sex. And would he stop talking about it? Would he heck.

At 8 pm another 'schoolgirl' arrived to the surprise of all the cronies and Ray and it all happened again, but no snogging at the end. Ray was in his element. Two in one night. What a result!

It was the talk of the school the next day and Ray boasted about it continually for the rest of his schooldays and no doubt when he went off to Hendon for his police training.

But, and here's the big but, I think it's time to confess to a little bit of skullduggery with regards to that night's events. You see, as I'd said before, we were fed up with Ray's continual apeman comments re: women and especially the less rugged males.

So I must admit it was me who arranged the first kissogram whom Ray snogged. It was a friend of mine called Simon who I believe still makes money in clubs as a female impersonator and, looks very good in a schoolgirl uniform. Comprendez?

Ray never actually changed and the last I heard he was on the beat somewhere in North London. At least I hope he listens to the breakfast show (I mean, who doesn't?).

I couldn't actually say anything at the time as the idea of my head and shoulders being detached didn't appeal to me but a good few of us knew and dropped subtle hints but they went way over Ray's head.

Now's the time to confess so I throw myself on the mercy of the court and jury and beg Dianne not to wear the black cap. After all I think Ray deserved it.

Yours in total subjection,
Kevin.

Dear Simon,

Every morning I look forward to the 'Confession' spot, and often drive to work with a smile on my face as I listen to another tale of mirthful sin. It is 'driving' that is the basis of this confession that happened about a year ago. To set the scene, I was working for a small design agency in Cambridge, for a real pig of a boss whom we shall call Swellhead. Now, Swellhead was about thirty years old, and had reached the top rung of the ladder in his profession so he thought it only fair that he should reward himself. To get to the top, he used the Mr Nasty Businessman school of thought, often resorting to threatening behaviour to get his own way! He chose to reward himself with not just any car; but a brand new, mean looking black RS Turbo. He started calling his car 'The Beast' as he often screamed around the local backroads 'eating up' other motorists.

Running into the office one day out of breath and in an obvious hurry, he ran into the studio, and threw his car keys at me, and told me to sling The Beast in the car park which was located behind the building, in front of the local supermarket. He then ran off into another part of the building to discuss technical matters with his biggest and richest client.

I dutifully walked to the front of the building and saw The Beast crouched temporarily on the kerbside on some double yellow lines. I climbed into The Beast, and sat for a while admiring the car, playing with the CD player before turning the key and starting the engine. Feeling pretty cool, I glanced around at passers-by as I lowered the electric window, and, as I was used to doing in my maroon Vauxhall Chevette, stamped my foot on the throttle. What happened next was a complete blur, as the car rocketed forward, I saw people leap aside as my nearside wheels mounted the kerb, and I careered into the entrance of the car park. I seem to remember the bulging eyes of a King Charles Spaniel, as it was wrenched from my path, and the startled face of an elderly lady, as she leaped aside as quickly as a sprightly eighteen-year-old! I steered towards an empty space, neglected to notice a shopping trolley on its side, and The Beast slewed to a sickening, metal-wrenching stop. Eventually I climbed out of the car to inspect the damage. I nearly collapsed when I saw a mangled shopping trolley protruding from the damaged front wheelarch.

Feeling very sick, I returned to the studio and quietly placed the keys back on his desk, and carried on with my work. I left early that day, before he was finished his meeting, and on my return the next morning Swellhead was nowhere to be seen! Asking a colleague about Swellhead's whereabouts, he told me that on returning to his car yesterday, and seeing the extensive damage, he flew into a blinding rage, and seeing a couple of kids playing shopping trolley dodgems had put two and two together and yanked a young lad from a trolley and threw him violently to the ground, screaming obscenities. The boy's father then emerged from the supermarket, and it wasn't until an off-duty policeman had arrived on the scene, that the fighting ceased, and Swellhead was dragged off to the police station.

I feel I must gain forgiveness from the small boy, who must have been scared witless by Swellhead in his rage, any passer-by that I narrowly missed, but most of all from the off-duty policeman who caught a nasty punch from Swellhead's windmilling arms, and gained a black eye into the bargain.

Jordan.

Dear Simon & the Crew,

This is not my own confession but a cracking tale about a local police sergeant which my husband heard about from a colleague. The sergeant was returning home from the station late one evening when he ran over a cat!

A few enquiries revealed it belonged to an old lady living nearby, so he went to her door, introduced himself and broke the bad news.

The poor old dear naturally was rather upset and the policeman did his best to comfort her. When she was calmer she asked if he could possibly bury the unfortunate animal for her at a nice spot nearby.

He promised faithfully and left after putting the deceased puss into a carrier bag in his boot, meaning to carry out the task in the morning.

On the Saturday his wife wanted to go shopping so they set off. While his wife got out of the car to pop into a shop in a quiet street the sergeant waited in the car and suddenly he remembered the cat – which was still in the boot!

Several days had passed and puss was by now not smelling his best, so the sergeant threw open the boot and stood well back. As he waited in the shop doorway he noticed a woman walk up to the car and quickly glance around her to see if anyone was looking. As the policeman looked on with a mixture of amazement and amusement the woman dived into the boot, nabbed the bag, took to her heels and ran!

Now the police sergeant couldn't resist the urge to follow her, not because she was a thief but to see if she'd look in the bag!

Sure enough just a little further up the street she stopped at a bus stop and took a peek. Next second she shrieked, reeled back, threw the bag over a wall and fainted in a heap!

So who needs more forgiveness here, the woman for being a thief or the sergeant for not arresting a criminal (although she probably learned her lesson) and more importantly for not burying the poor old lady's cat, which is still probably lying at the bottom of someone's garden in Aberdeen.

Love,
Donna.

Dear Father Simon, Sister Dianne and Brother Rod,
Please can you help me purge my soul and conscience of the memory of two events that happened on the same day in 1972 when I was a police officer in a large constabulary in the North of England?

The first event probably demonstrates what planks the police employed at that time, but the second . . . well, words fail me . . .

One morning I was late for work and on arriving at 6.30 am instead of 6.00 am I was rewarded with the job of giving the prisoners their breakfasts.

We had to collect the breakfasts from the fire station across the road and it always consisted of a large jug of steaming tea and some hot bacon sandwiches. Down I merrily went into the cell block with the tea etc. and went into a cell which was set aside for sorting out the prisoners' meals – pouring out the tea into cups and putting the sandwiches on plates. As I entered the cell I kicked the cell door behind me (hoping just to close it slightly) and heart it gently shut and of course the lock engage. My heart sank. Not to worry, I thought, I've got a very large bunch of keys with me for all the cell doors.

I then realized that cell doors don't in fact have a keyhole on the inside (I was only young at the time) and so for the next twenty minutes wondered what to do. In desperation I decided to press the alarm button and had to be rescued by a fellow officer whom I swore to silence.

As for the prisoners' breakfasts – well by this time the tea was stone cold and the bacon sandwiches horribly congealed, so I would like to confess to the prisoners that it was in fact my fault and that I was being *slightly* economical with the truth when I told them loudly, 'Sorry lads but those prats at the fire station couldn't organize a . . . etc.' But worse was to follow!

Later the same morning I spotted on the police station notice board details of a parade by Scouts and Guides that day and realized that I was supposed to be on point-duty at a particularly busy road junction to stop the traffic for the parade about 10 minutes later. I left the station rapidly and arrived at this junction just in time to confirm on my radio that I was in position.

Shortly I heard the sound of bugles and kazoos approaching and could see about 100 Scouts and Guides marching up the road towards me. At this point I suddenly realized that I had read the notice in the Police Station so quickly that I didn't have a clue which way the march was supposed to go at my junction. Common sense would have told you that they would probably be heading for the town centre, but at that moment any common sense which I had went straight out of the window.

What did I do? Well naturally I stopped all the traffic and directed the parade straight up the dual carriageway towards the M62 Motorway! Seeing the youngsters march off into the distance I did what anyone would have done under the circumstances. I legged it, Father Simon, reappearing at the police station some hours later with a severe case of 'Sorry, Sergeant, but these radio batteries are useless, they don't last ten minutes now'.

Now maybe the prisoners' breakfasts fiasco wasn't the end of the world. But I have this recurring image of a group of about 100 ten- to fourteen-year-olds – our future generation – possibly being mowed down by a juggernaut and all my fault. Only you can forgive this transgression. Help me, Father, for I have sinned.

Yours repentantly,
An Ex-Police Officer.

Dear Father Mayo and The Forgiveness Panel,

I must seek absolution for the following, which occurred in the summer of 1990. I am a military police dog handler and at the time was serving at several bases in Western Europe, I'd made friends with Maria, who lived near one particular base, and I used to 'pop round most evenings to make sure she was OK'.

Maria had recently bought Rambo, an Alsatian dog who had been abandoned at the local dogs' home, he proved to be badly behaved and Maria had been taking him to obedience classes for weeks without much success. One evening she came home in tears; the instructor had finally lost patience with Rambo and told Maria that unless Rambo's behaviour improved dramatically, the following week would be the last for both of them. They were humiliated in front of all the other dogs and handlers.

Clearly, Simon, some sort of revenge was required and that night, influenced by several lagers, a plan was formulated. The following week I took the dog to the class, where he behaved perfectly, obeying all the instructor's directions, much to his disbelief. However the instructor wasn't convinced that it was a permanent improvement so I said, 'I've been teaching him to be a guard dog, would you like a demonstration?'

The instructor simply laughed and said, 'That dog could never guard anything.' Simon, that was the cue for action. I wish to confess that the Alsatian with the unusually large teeth that pinned the instructor to the ground with his jaws around the poor man's neck was not Rambo but Muax, my highly trained and slightly psychotic guard dog who has been trained to bite hard without breaking the skin.

I'm told the teethmarks stayed for several days on the instructor's neck and he became a nervous wreck, especially near Alsatians. But revenge was sweet. Rambo is just as unruly now but I think justice was done. Can the panel forgive me for illegal use of a lethal weapon? I must remain anonymous for obvious reasons.

Yours in hope,
The Phantom Policeman.

Monsignor Mayo and Holy Helpers,

The beginnning of my deceitfulness goes back to 1974, just after I had left the Merchant Navy. As the saying goes 'any port in a storm' and it is in the port of Cardiff that my indiscretion occurred. Being a sailor, or in my case an ex-sailor, there is usually a girl involved. In my private life at that time the young lady in question was the daughter of a high ranking police officer.

To say that he wasn't enamoured about my relationship with his daughter was an understatement. Given the choice he would have willingly locked me in a cell and thrown away the key. All because he thought that I was uneducated and only after one thing as far as his daughter was concerned.

In order to try and get my feet under the table, so to speak, I used to visit on a Sunday afternoon. Unfortunately it always corresponded with the time that 'University Challenge' was on the TV. For the first three weeks you can imagine how I felt not being able to answer correctly any of the questions. This just went down really well with her father, proving as far as he was concerned that I *was* uneducated.

As the weeks progressed you can imagine my dilemma, and then my opportunity to prove otherwise (revenge) came to me like a truncheon out of the blue.

Where they lived in Cardiff they could only receive 'University Challenge' two days later than most of the country, so one Friday I diligently watched the programme at home and on Sunday, armed with all the answers, I arrived at Château Wormwood Scrubs.

Settling down, me with a smug smile on my face, we all prepared to watch the ritual programme. So as not to arouse suspicion, for the first few questions I kept up my normal act. At the first opportunity, when Mr Plod had answered incorrectly, in I came with the right answer. Okay, for the first couple of times they regarded it as sheer luck, but as time went by his contemptuous remarks changed to remarks of wonderment and respect.

Over the next few weeks I played my part to the full, dropping in wrong answers and changing my mind at the last minute to get them right.

As you can imagine Mr Plod's thoughts towards me gradually changed and I was accepted as part of the family and a prospective son-in-law. I'm sorry to say that it didn't work out that way as I started going round on Thursdays when 'Mastermind' was on and I got rumbled.

I don't seek forgiveness for my dreadful deceit but for the fact that whilst there I neglected his daughter and that I now can't even remember their names. So it just goes to show how important an event it was in my life.

Yours hopefully,
John.

Dear Father Simon, Choirboy Rod, and Mother Superior Dianne,

By the time this letter reaches you it will have missed your request for police confessions, but after listening to the letters last week I felt compelled to confess on behalf of a friend.

To set the scene my friend, whom we'll call Bob, failed to achieve the required grades to enter medical school, so in a search for a career with 'action' applied for and successfully joined our local county constabulary.

After four months intense training the obligatory attendance at an autopsy was called for at a local hospital. On hearing this Bob enthused at the opportunity to view some real 'action'.

During the previous four months one particular member of the class had been the ultimate pain in the proverbial, and a loud one at that, quickly obtaining the nickname Blackwall Gob. Blackwall had quickly started his boasting 'I've-seen-it/done-it-all-before . . .' attitude when he was informed of the pending hospital outing.

Both Bob and the instructor of the class had both quietly aired their opinions of what they thought of Blackwall, and so seeing the mortuary visit as a perfect opportunity to verbally castrate the mighty mouth, started plotting. The day arrived and 26 pasty faces alighted from the police van and entered the mortuary department. The doctor scheduled to lecture the group was still finishing off a customer (sorry!) and so the group was asked to wait in an anteroom out the back of the main theatre. This room led off to the refrigerated room where the body drawers were situated. Bob and the instructor pulled Blackwall to the side and asked him if he would like to help play a joke on the rest of the unsuspecting class. Of course he grabbed the chance. They said he should lie in one of the body drawers with a sheet over him and then when the doctor showed the class around he would pull out the relevant drawer and then Blackwall could sit up and frighten the rest of the class. We duly stripped him of uniform down to his Y-fronts and laid him to rest!

To make it clear to those of you who are unfamiliar with a mortuary drawer, when the drawers are pushed back in, the fridge is open plan. That is to say when Blackwall was pushed back in, he could look either side of him and see all the other 'residents'!

They assured Blackwall that he would only be in there for two or three minutes . . . They knew that after ten minutes one of two things would happen – either he would start shouting and banging to get out, or he would mutter something like 'For goodness sake hurry up . . .'

Well the latter occurred, as planned, and this is where a strategically placed second person came into play! Another 'keen to quieten Blackwall' candidate had offered his services. He lay in an adjacent drawer and in reply to Blackwall's lonely (or so he thought) mutter replied, 'Cold in here, isn't it?'

To say that the screams from Blackwall Gob could have woken the dead is not an overstatement, and to say he was introverted after the prank is perfectly true.

I would like to beg forgiveness for Bob and his instructor, but also for the likes of myself who thinks the prank hilarious but quite rightly cruel.

Yours requesting absolution,
Natalie.

5

All In A Day's Work

This section is dedicated to the following people, without whom it would not have been possible: the office joker, the office romeo, the practical joker, the jobsworth and the office snob. Thank you. May you live long and prosper.

Dear Simon and the rest of the gang,

My confession concerns a job where I was secretary to the sales director of a well-known underwear company some years ago.

Because of the product we manufactured, i.e. bras and knickers, etc., it was the norm for the table at board meetings to be covered with new products and for bras to be passed around the table so each director could feel the new elastic or stretchability, etc. It was also not unusual for me to have to engage a couple of models to parade in the underwear so that everyone could see what it looked like in situ. This is all just scene-setting.

On one particular day we had a very important board meeting with visiting directors from our main office in Paris and other continental offices. We all had to be on very best behaviour and give the impression of efficiency.

The dignitaries arrived and were closeted in the boardroom at the end of the corridor so we could all breathe again for a short while. It so happened that that afternoon Margaret, one of the secretaries, had had a new typist's chair delivered which was a super-duper effort with castors, hydraulic pump-action seat and everything a typist dreams of. She tried it out and was well impressed. We all were. What were the castors like, though, did they glide? We set out to find out. She wheeled herself around a little, but to get the proper 'feel' we decided it would be better if we wheeled her . . .

We started at the very end of the corridor. I pushed Margaret faster and faster down the corridor until we got up a real speed – those castors certainly worked well. She approached the boardroom door with every intention of slowing down long before, but no, the speed was so great she couldn't stop easily and as I had let go and dived into one of the offices she was speeding along like a good-un. At that precise moment my boss, the Sales Director, opened the boardroom door to show out the visitors as the meeting had finished. Margaret sailed in, legs in the air, straight into the wonderful table display of bras, knickers and the like. Embarrassment all round, no excuses, lots of apologies and red faces. I had long gone and just appeared to enquire what the noise was!

I would like to apologise to Margaret who got the severe telling off 'for behaving in such a childish manner' and hadn't she got something better to do? To my boss, Ken, who was out to set a really good example of how the English office was run, and to the amazed important visitors who never knew what had hit them. Forgiveness please (it was great fun at the time though).

Maureen.

Dear Simon,

I ask forgiveness for an incident that happened a number of years ago when I was just a slip of a secretary.

I was working for a London-based company who had recently opened a regional office in Manchester, housed in a smart suite of offices opposite Piccadilly railway station. My boss was a smarmy ex-copier salesman of the worst kind. (If you've ever met a copier salesman you'll know the type.) He was married to a lovely, smiley girl and they had a delightful two-year-old boy.

As we were a new business we weren't exactly run off our feet and my Boss, whom I called The Rat, started to take longer and longer lunch hours returning to the office happier and happier with a succession of fluffy blondes for coffee, which they took in one of the spare offices behind locked doors.

The coffee must have been delicious judging from the appreciative noises although it was only a cheap instant brand and not one, I would have thought, to get worked up over. It was bad enough having to listen to them enjoying their 'coffee' but he expected me to fend off telephone callers and cover for him. I sat silently fuming and plotting his downfall.

One afternoon I had taken the phone off the hook so that he would not be disturbed during his 'coffee' and was making my way to the ladies when I saw his wife, toddler by the hand, arriving in the lift. This was my chance! But one look at her happy, smiling face and I knew I couldn't be so heartless. I palmed her off with a story that Superboss had arrived from London and it would be inconvenient – she took the hint and left.

Back in the office I decided that was IT! Enough was enough. The Rat had to go!

Fate intervened the next day while The Rat was having one of his lunches. Superboss rang and said he was taking the train to see us the next afternoon and would be arriving about 2.30 pm. I calculated that the timing would be perfect and The Rat would be deeply engrossed in his 'coffee'. Naturally, when The Rat returned from his lunch all happy, goodwill oozing out of his ratlike features, I somehow 'forgot' to tell him of the impending visit.

There were no leaves on the line that day and at 2.35 precisely Superboss arrived. The Rat was enjoying himself so much he did not hear him patronize his way past my desk and head to the main office. His attention was arrested by the strange sounds issuing from the spare office and he stopped in his tracks and tried the door. There was a deathly silence and as he shook the handle he shouted, 'Open this door AT ONCE!' The ensuing panic was almost audible.

The memory of the two of them, The Rat and the by now not-so-fluffy blonde, scuttling out of the office in complete disarray has kept me warm over many a long winter evening.

Needless to say, I never saw The Rat again and the very next week I had a new unmarried boss who shared his afternoon coffee with ME.

Yours penitently,
Miss Smith.

Dear Father Mayo, Brother Rod and Sister Dianne,

I spent many happy hours working for our own local Hospital Radio station, which was quite an impressive set-up compared to some. The programmes were networked to all the hospitals in and around the city, and therefore commanded quite a large potential audience. Bearing this in mind, most people, myself no exception, were nervous when first confronted with a microphone. Our training was quite comprehensive, and included making a pilot programme for our beloved Programmes Controller to listen to, before we were let loose 'on the air'.

After a few years, I decided to get more involved in the technical side of things, and have a go at operating all the switches, faders and knobs, and actually putting on the records, tapes and jingles and things, which was normally done for us by a technical operator. Once again the old tummy-butterflies got to work the first time I did this for a live programme, but, with loads of practice, I became quite proficient and blasé. As seasoned operators, one of our functions was to look after the new recruits, and help them through their training period, and generally put them at their ease, which brings me to my confession.

Anybody that has ever worked in either hospital or any kind of radio will have encountered the likes of Kevin, one of the new trainees. (Name changed!!) He thought he was God's gift to broadcasting, and was really doing us a favour by slumming it in our little Hospital Radio station until a suitable vacancy occurred on Radio 1. Despite his apparent loud and arrogant manner, it became obvious that even he was not immune to a touch of nerves when confronted with a microphone in the deathly silence of a soundproofed studio. When I discovered that I would be doing the operating for Kevin's pilot programme, my plot to take him down a peg or three was hatched.

The first four minutes went quite well all things considered, with perhaps the exception of his slightly trembling voice. Then, as our intrepid presenter was halfway through his next link, I quietly informed him (again over talkback so nobody else could hear) that the stylus had broken on the turntable, and could he keep talking whilst I fixed it.

Anybody who has ever tried this will know that it is at best extremely difficult to talk intelligibly for more than a minute or so when you are not expecting to have to do so, so I let him burble away about the weather, his auntie's budgie and his holiday last year in Torremolinos for a full seven minutes whilst I busily pretended to fix the broken stylus. I finally put him out of his misery by whispering 'It's OK, I'm ready now!' through his headphones. He looked positively relieved as his second record started. However, his relief was to be short-lived – my fun had only just begun!

As his record was about halfway through, I flipped the switch that cut off his headphones. Puzzled by the sudden silence, he began waving wildly to attract my attention. I pretended not to notice, and, as the studio was soundproofed his cries of protest went unheeded. Again, as his record began to fade, the sound of his headphones was miraculously restored. He bumbled and fluffed his way through the next link, and, when the next record was under way, he asked me what had happened. I smiled sweetly and asked what on earth he was talking about, as everything was fine in the control room.

I allowed the next couple of records and links to proceed without a hitch, just to lull our Kevin into a false sense of security. Time now for the pièce de résistance! Whilst his final record was playing away merrily, I flipped a few switches on the control desk in such a way that, when he next spoke through the microphone, he would hear his own voice through his headphones, but with a one second delay. I sat back and eagerly awaited his final link. I opened his microphone, and fought to keep a straight face as he vainly struggled to speak intelligibly, hearing his own words one second after he had spoken them. The effect was quite devastating as he garbled and stammered his way through the wind up of his pilot programme. Again I smiled sweetly and innocently as, having emerged from the studio a broken man, he enquired what the heck had happened. I denied all knowledge of any problems with the recording, and played him back a bit of his tape to prove it . . .

Kevin departed from Hospital Radio shortly afterwards, and has not been seen or heard of since.

Yours sincerely,
Paul.

Dear Father Mayo,
I ask forgiveness for something which happened in the summer of 1981 at a small place called Kussell in Southern Germany.

At the time I was employed as a sound engineer with a well known Sixties band called ----- and Titch. I think you know who I mean. (Zabadack.)

We were coming to the end of an exceptionally arduous tour of 40 one-night shows when we came to Kussell. The last but one night of the tour everything went well and the band ended up with a standing ovation. As the club was a disco we decided not to wait until 3 am to clear away the equipment but to get on with it straight away. Having stacked it all by the door I decided to go and get the van. So I went outside to a particularly dark car park, jumped in the van and started to reverse. This was when I realized something was wrong with the brakes, because no matter how hard I revved the engine the van only moved at a snail's pace. It was as if something was holding me back. At this point I got that terrible sinking feeling. Had I checked behind the van before moving off?

As quickly as I could I drove the van back to its original resting place and walked back to investigate.

To my horror I found this beautiful brand new black 845 Alpina BMW with a totally rearranged bonnet and nearside wing. I ran into the club and got hold of the drummer and told him what had happened. After much earbashing and general abuse we devised a cunning plan. We observed that the vast majority of the audience were totally legless and surmised that the owner of the BMW would drive home and on waking the next morning think, 'Blimey, I don't remember doing that!' So we waited and we waited but to no avail, the car just sat there so we decided to ask the DJ to announce, 'Would the owner of the black BMW please move it?' but he said no need as it was the club owner's car. Well the club owner came out and gave the keys to one of his bar staff, telling him to move it, which this big blond German bloke did. Well, we quickly loaded the van and fled.

The next morning we were sat outside the hotel having breakfast when we saw the BMW come down the hill and pull up. The club owner jumped out and explained that the idiot of a barman had wrecked his pride and joy and had we witnessed anything. Well we of course shook our heads in disbelief at what the barman had done and tried to console the grieving owner. That night we packed up at breakneck speed and made a dash for the border.

I now feel I should ask for your forgiveness and hope the barman found himself another job and place to live.

Yours sorrowfully,
A very embarrassed sound engineer.

Dear Father Mayo and Clerical Clan,

My confession is one that recounts a despicable act which deprived a close friend of fame and fortune. It is a story of avarice and deception; of betrayal and contempt; of a friendship that developed into a feud.

It all began many years ago when I was first cast into the wide world to earn my living. I had decided that I would support myself and my nocturnal habits with the aid of a pen. I would be a writer.

I moved into an apartment near Cheltenham with a close friend who also saw his destiny guided by the scribblings of a fully loaded quill. Our mutual interest in the theatre and writing sustained a friendship that was to last for several years. It was not long after moving in that we read in the local journal that a new theatre was to be built nearby, and that a new thespian group was in search of previously unpublished plays to perform at the new venue. Francis and I set to work.

Before long it had become obvious to me that my friend was blessed with much more talent than myself. His writings flowed where mine merely dribbled. Our initial submissions were judged to be almost perfect; his perfect, . . . mine almost! I was shattered, my whole future, my entire purpose in life, lay in tatters on the floor of the new theatre.

Francis continued to write. He wrote of young love between feuding families; of fairy realms and human intruders; of monarchs and merchants. The stories flowed from his pen as if it were possessed. He had been given a deadline within which to produce the plays and he completed the last one on the eve of that deadline.

It was at this juncture that I betrayed my friend. That night, while he slept, I substituted his works for my own. The following day when he submitted the plays to the Thespians, he was not to know that the work was that of an untalented amanuensis. The critics read the work and with one voice ridiculed my friend and banished him from the theatre.

When the fuss had died down I stepped forward with the original manuscripts and professed that they were my own work. The critics loved the plays and within weeks they were being performed before capacity audiences. My fame was assured, my fortune guaranteed, I thought. I went on to write more and more. It was all rubbish but nobody had the guts to tell me so. My reputation was made by those first manuscripts.

I beg forgiveness for the initial deceit; for betraying my friend and subjecting him to criticism that ruined his life and deprived him of a fortune; for subjecting students worldwide to terms of absolute purgatory when trying to understand my later works, and most of all, for taking up your valuable time with this utter nonsense.

Yours in hope of eternal peace,
Billy Wagastick.

Dear Father Simon, Sister Di and Brother Rod,

I would like to free myself of a burden that I have carried with me since 1987.

I was when I had the exquisite pleasure of working on a fresh fish counter in a large supermarket, which shall remain nameless as I wouldn't want to offend Gateway.

The job entailed a very early start, at 7 am, when we (me and my two chums) would completely fill the eighteen foot counter with crushed ice, which was mass produced by a very temperamental ice maker in the prep. room, then laying out, in a very beautiful display, all sorts of fish, some whole some filleted and some sliced. The displays were our pride and joy, scenes of fish eating smaller ones, salmon swirling in spirals (Rod should like that one!) and smoked fish in wide fan shapes, all dotted with bunches of parsley and slices of lemon.

However, the centre of the service counter was raised higher than the rest and at an angle of 30° and had to have whole fresh rainbow trout in vertical rows covering the entire centre piece. Now, this looked fine albeit lacking in imagination, so we decided to liven it up a bit – literally!!

One day, when business was slower than usual and boredom was setting in, I came up with the perfect way to brighten our day.

I managed to obtain a very long piece of wire from another department and carefully hooking the end into a trout's eye I ran the wire under the head, under the ice, over the top of the counter and along the back to the end, where I stood looking bored and uninterested (as is required of most supermarket staff!!).

The wire was completely out of sight of the customers and so when a young family approached, the wicked but hilarious plan went into action.

As often happens in supermarkets, the adults were chatting, oblivious to their little darlings exploits, and so the sight of whole, slimy, wet fish, eyes and all, was irresistible to one little boy who came over to have a closer look. Just, as his hot little hand came within a trout's nose's distance of the fish, I jerked the wire and the head twitched perfectly in mock death throes.

I have several points on which I would like to be forgiven:-

1. for putting the parents in an embarrassing position of having to calm down a near-hysterical child in the middle of a supermarket.

2. from the child who received a rather hefty whack for telling lies about the trout, who, incidentally, had suddenly and mysteriously become inert once again.

3. And finally from the trout, whose life ended only to be a party to my evil fishing frolics.

Lots of Love and fishy fingers,
Jan.

Dear Simon,

At certain times of the month, when I get a bit low and fed up with life, nature turns me into a cross between the child in 'The Exorcist' and a tearful wimp; I'm not pleasant company! I'm also several sizes bigger than usual, due to fluid retention.

Not so long ago, feeling pretty low and decidedly ugly, I thought I'd cheer myself up. Now, not being particularly rational at this time I thought I'd go and try on some clothes. I went round a few shops and, feeling a bit like a king size waterbed, got extremely angry when clothes normally two sizes too big, wouldn't fit and wouldn't even do up!

I was skiving from work and therefore still in my suit. During the afternoon several women had actually come up to me in shops assuming I worked there. It was then that my cunning plan entered my head.

I chose a shop with one of these changing rooms situated at the back, tucked away and unsupervised. As it was close to closing time all the assistants were standing by the front door with an armful of clothes giggling inanely every time they accidentally set off the alarm and not paying attention to anything. I stood outside the changing room of this particular shop – occasionally adjusting the unwanted clothes on the rack until a 'size 10' walked up with some items she wanted to try on . . .

'Is it OK if I try these on?' she squeaked.

'No, sorry, we're only letting in the more normal sizes after 3 o'clock from now on to try and shift some stock. Now, if you were a size 14 or 16 you'd be OK.' Miss 'Size 10' stared at me in disbelief but contemplating my hulking great frame decided against arguing. This continued for about fifteen minutes – letting in big sizes with a smile and turning away anyone remotely thin – when I decided to quit while I was ahead and walked out of the shop with a smile and a song in my heart.

I do not seek forgiveness from any of the customers – anyone who has a waistline of less than 27 inches deserves everything they get. However, I would like to apologize to the shop for potential loss of sales in this time of hardship for retailers – so what do you say?

Yours,
Jenny.

Dear Simon,

Time has come for me to confess my sins.

This particular one takes us back to the summer of '86 when, as every summer, I was earning – working very, very hard – lots of money working as a lifeguard in an American military base in Naples. Life was hard and very, very hot! That morning the swimming pool had been particularly crowded and Jeremy, a colleague lifeguard, and I were very tired and more sunburned than usual.

Around 6 pm the Head Lifeguard told us that he was going to leave a bit earlier that day and he asked Jeremy and me if we would mind closing up. The thrill of being in charge overcame us. 'Of course not,' was the proud reply. 'One last recommendation before I go,' the boss said. 'Don't forget to turn the water off before you leave.' To those that are not too familiar with swimming pools, the refilling water is very cold.

At 6.30, we received a phone call inviting us to a party, but we had to be ready by 7 pm. 'We'll be there!' was the quick reply. The party was great fun.

The morning after, and believe me it was one, Jeremy and I had an early start. When we got there we received a big shock. The pool was overflowing! We'd forgotten to turn the water off.

We started emptying the pool with plastic buckets but that wasn't enough. The water was freezing. We turned the heating on, but that wasn't enough either. At 9 o'clock the first customer arrived. It was Col. 'X', a retired 68-year-old gentleman, who every morning came to the pool before the crowd arrives for his 50 lengths.

Jeremy and I looked at each other with horror. 'If he goes in, he'll die,' Jeremy said.

He approached the diving board, looked at the water, bounced once . . . twice . . . stopped. When we thought we'd got away with it, he dived! We rushed to the side of the pool and stared at him lying down at the bottom of the pool.

'He's not moving,' I said.

'Jump in,' Jeremy replied.

'You go,' was my response.

About thirty seconds later, we got him out with a hook which was used in case of emergencies. 'He's alive!!!' we both cheered.

'The water,' he shouted, 'is . . . is . . . cold!!'

'No, sir, you probably had something to eat which upset your system.'

The manager shut the pool because the water was too cold and we had to take a day off. We also got away with it as the Head Lifeguard got the blame.

I would like to ask your forgiveness as well as that of all those customers who were turned away on a very, very hot day of August.

Yours sincerely,
Marcello.

Dear Boys and Girl,

I'd like to take this opportunity to unburden myself of double guilt in the art of window-dressing . . .

Window-Dressing #1

I was working at a now-bust photo store as a 'junior' (or as everyone else knows it, a 'gopher'). My duties included going to the bank with the takings for the night safe.

The shop was double-fronted, with photographic goods in one window and optical gear in the other. The shop owner's idea of modern equipment was interesting but I put forward the idea to exhibit photographs of mine in the window to 'show how good our processing services were'. I was actually touting for freelance jobs. The photographic window looked brilliant.

No so, the optical goods window. The gear for there had lousy subjects for an artist such as myself to show off: The quality goods were so expensive that a casual buyer wouldn't want them anyway and the affordable stuff was cheap-and-nasty to say the least! What could be done to make this window interesting? Most of the shop's clients were 'no spring chickens'. Why didn't I make things easier to see?

One of the popular bits of kit was a magnifying glass on a flexible arm – the sort of thing model-makers might use. This could be put to better use . . . The window was organized and a nice bed of velvet was freshly shaken to use as a bed for everything on display. The binoculars were assembled into one of the most spectacular displays the shop had seen in a long time and the name of them could be clearly seen through the magnifying glass. Clever?

Not so. I hadn't taken account of the *movement* of the earth. By the afternoon the display was certainly attracting more than its fair share of onlookers – but only one wandered in, *quite casually*, and offered. 'Do you know your window display's on fire?' The sun's beams were being focused by the glass and the velvet was in flames . . .

I'd like too ask forgiveness for this – though it was more an *act of the gods* than my fault. Perhaps I should have considered that the clouds might not be around all day (but it was in Edinburgh!) and that something like this might happen — but no harm came of it and it did brighten up an otherwise boring day.

Window-dressing #2

A friend of mine and I were engrossed in assembling glass and china in another Edinburgh store.

The chap I was with was one of the directors of the shop's parent company and we could call him Charlie. His name.

The task we had was to dress the shelving in the three shop windows. Nothing could be simpler — and nothing more boring, either!

When we were arranging one window, people outside came to see what was on offer. Now, rather than moving out of the way for them to see, we 'froze'. This was quite difficult to begin with as we were usually standing awkwardly in the first place but we gradually got better and other folk soon realized we were part of the display. How clever . . .

How clever indeed: One particularly successful time that we 'froze' I happened to be looking at the female in the pairing outside. She looked right at me, expecting nothing, and was greeted with a wink!

Her face was a picture. How *I* managed *not* to smile escapes me, but I continued to stand stony-faced, staring right at her. She'd grabbed her mate with such ferocity that I was amazed they didn't try to come into what was obviously a shut shop. She was trying to explain what had happened and this explanation was being fobbed off. Her partner went to look at the next window, hands shaking dismissively. Charlie and I had managed to stand still for over five minutes by now and the woman was going to go off unbelieved. Poor thing, eh?

The couple left having looked at what Nisbet's (the shop) was going to offer when they opened. But she just had to have one last look — isn't it always the way? She turned to stare at me and I never flinched. As she was *just* leaving she had yet another sideways glance at me — and I waved my fingers slightly and grinned . . .

I'd like to ask forgiveness for upsetting this poor woman in the first place but I did let her go off knowing that I was real after all, so no harm was done in the end. Am I, and Charlie, forgiven?

Yours sincerely,
Nik.

Dear Simon, Brother Rod and Sister Di,

The story I am about to relate took place in December 1978. At the time I was a milkman in Nottingham working for a well known dairy.

I began my round at about 5 each morning and at about 7.30 I would call on an elderly gent whom I shall call Bert. Unfortunately, Bert was housebound due to age and illness and so I took it upon myself to make both Bert and myself a cup of tea each morning.

On the morning in question Bert said, 'Do you like brazil nuts?' I replied, 'Indeed I do.' 'Great', said Bert, 'on the sideboard is a bag of brazils. Please take them with my compliments.' After thanking him I said 'see you tomorrow,' and carried on with my deliveries.

At about midday I arrived back at the depot and having first unloaded my empties I made my way to the rest room to count my daily takings and cash them in. As I was doing so I suddenly remembered the bag of brazil nuts I had left in my float and so as a gesture of goodwill I went to fetch them and handed them to the five girls working in the office. Within seconds the whole bag had been devoured, not one nut remained for myself or my fellow roundsman.

At about 7.30 am the next morning I arrived at Bert's house and proceeded to make our daily cuppa. Suddenly Bert said, 'Did you enjoy the brazil nuts?' To which I replied, 'I gave them to the girls in the office and they all send their thanks and best wishes.'

Bert's next words will remain with me for ever. 'Originally, you know, they were chocolate brazils. I sucked the chocolate off. But I can't eat the nuts because they get under the plate of my false teeth.'

For the next four hours I was in a daze, I couldn't wait to get back to the depot and relate the conversation to all my fellow roundsmen and also the girls in the office.

Simon, I beg forgiveness for roundsmen having to wait for over two hours to cash in their takings until the green-gilled cashiers appeared from the ladies' rooom.

Best regards,
Keith.

Dear Simon,

Back in the early 1970s I started a job as a pollution control officer looking after a large well-known river in central Scotland (which rhymes with Slide). Jobs were hard to come by and the River Purification Board set very high standards for their employees – in fact they made it abundantly clear to me that if I didn't perform miracles during my six months probationary period, I'd be out on my ear. I was desperate to impress so the word 'failure' was eradicated from my dictionary.

One of my first jobs was to investigate the source of minor oil contamination of the pristine upper reaches of this magnificent river. I quickly traced it to a drainage pipe in the river bank but couldn't easily establish which of three nearby oil-using premises was discharging the oil into this pipe. I dared not return to my headquarters without being able to report that I had traced and stopped the oil – especially as the local radio station and newspapers were pressuring my boss for a statement about the incident. I knew that one sure-fire way of testing if a premises was connected to a particular pipe, was to put a special harmless dye into a drain at the premises and see if the colour turned up in the pipe at the river – simple as that!

I had a gallon of concentrated fluorescent red dye in my van for just this purpose, so I set to work at once. I unscrewed the stopper and thought, 'Hmmmm, I've never used this stuff before . . . I wonder how much I should use?' To play safe, I just poured in half a cupful but when, after waiting an hour, the colour hadn't appeared at the river, I decided to slosh the whole gallon in.

Ten minutes later an incredible garish red colour spouted forth into the river from the drain, which turned the entire width of the river pale pink for about fifteen minutes before fading away to nothing. What a shock I had, but after regaining my composure, I felt quietly pleased with myself and marched confidently into the polluter's premises and gave them a right royal rollicking and got them to stop the cause of the oil discharge immediately.

I returned to the river bank in the certain knowledge that the oily discharge should have stopped and the river should have been perfect again.

Well, the oil had stopped . . . but it wasn't perfect – it was blinding red in colour. The sunlight reflecting off it lit the whole valley up a rosy red – miles and miles of a gigantic fluorescent scarlet ribbon winding its way through one of the most beautiful landscapes in Britain. I realized what I had done – the first wee drop of dye caused the river to turn pink and an hour behind it came a whole gallon – it was just like the film 'The Ten Commandments' when Moses dipped his staff into the sea.

As I mentioned earlier, the dye was harmless, but that was no consolation to thousands of pink fish, and owners of pink rowing boats, and several farmers who owned pink and black sheepdogs and cattle with pink legs and heads.

Best wishes,
Chris.

Dear Father Mayo,

My 'crime' took place about nine years ago, when a friend and I decided to go out for a curry and a few beers on a Saturday night. No harm in that really, but on the way to the restaurant we had to walk past an art gallery.

Ordinarily, we wouldn't have given the art gallery a second glance, but on this particular night, it was apparent that those people visiting the gallery were being given free wine. Can you imagine that? All you had to do was to look at some boring paintings and you were given a glass of wine, free!

So, in we went. Well, it would have been rude not to, really. We collected our free glass of wine and started to show a marginal interest in the 'works of art' on display. The longer we stayed, the more wine we received.

It dawned on us that some of the other guests were seriously interested in some of the paintings, and clearly enjoyed expressing their views to each other. So we thought we'd join in. The wine had made us particularly vociferous and we were soon debating the various merits of the artist's work with the other guests.

I am unable to explain why, but some of the other guests seemed to believe the rubbish we were spouting and started to ask our opinions on individual works which the artist was displaying. One particularly nice old lady did ask me why I was attending this function, and so I told her, 'I am the art critic from Country Life.' Amazingly she believed me and insisted on my pointing out my personal favourites to her, which I willingly did.

I was famous and enjoying it until I was approached by a lady (I think her name was Anne Masters?) who said, 'I understand you're from Country Life?'

'That's correct,' I lied.

'Nice to meet you, I'm (Anne Masters?). I'm the art critic from The Guardian'.

My cover was blown, I thought, although I did converse with my fellow critic for some time and even she seemed to believe me. I don't doubt, there is probably an (Anne Masters?) telling this same story in reverse somewhere.

Now, in between the drinking and lying, my friend and I noticed that each work of art was either marked by a yellow or a red sticker. Basically, red stickers meant the work had been sold, and yellow meant it was still for sale. Isn't it amazing, but at that point in time, it seemed like the only thing to do was to switch the stickers around to cause absolute confusion. So we did.

Despite all this, we were still welcome to stay at the gallery because we were very much the centre of attention. 'The art critic from Country Life and his friend were more than welcome to have more wine', explained the gallery manager. 'However, we are running low, and we are open for the rest of the weekend.'

'No problem,' explained my friend (Paul). 'My father owns an off licence, and is driving down to Cheltenham tonight to meet us for dinner. I'll ask him to bring a case of wine, which of course, we will pay for.' Paul picked up the phone and dialled the speaking clock and held a conversation with his 'father' detailing our requirements. 'The wine will be here in one hour, we'll be back later,' we lied again, as we staggered off into town.

Naturally, we have never returned to the said gallery, with or without a case of wine. I am sorry, on reflection, for the chaos caused by our lying, drinking and swapping of labels, which resulted in four paintings being sold twice and a lot of shouting. However, I don't expect forgiveness from anyone, especially Dianne. I just thought I'd write in and tell you about it.

Yours artistically,
Mark.

6

Too Close For Comfort

Being on your own in life is not a state sought by many. Mind you, there are some advantages. Just think: no one to laugh at your cock-ups, no one to steal your boyfriend/girlfriend/pets/sherbert lemons, report you to the police, etc. Become a hermit – it's safer than being surrounded by families and friends like these . . .

Dear Simon,

This confession is on behalf of two friends of mine, Phil and Rod. They don't seem to feel in the least bit guilty about it, in fact they seem to find it rather funny, but I will let you be the judge.

The story begins at the local town's rugby club post-defeat celebration. Our two heroes started chatting up two local girls who, for once, chatted back. Now Phil and Rod would not have full dance cards at a Neanderthal Hallowe'en Ball, but the girls appeared to enjoy their company and the evening started to go with a swing. Closing time came and the offer of a cup of coffee back at Rod's place was accepted.

Rod at this time lived in his parents' house, a large and rambling place out in the sticks. What happened in the lounge that night was a little hazy, but after a few cups of coffee, a long and intense debate on philosophical methods, and a certain amoung of rather juvenile rummaging around, the girls called a cab and left. Phil and Rod then staggered to bed with self-satisfied smirks on their faces.

The next day the lounge looked as if Motorhead had trashed it. Strewn around the floor were cushions, unwashed cups, cigarette ends, and small pieces of shredded material that looked suspiciously like the remains of a pair of tights. In the middle of the floor was a pair of rather distinctive red shoes that one of the girls must have left in her hurry to get away from the gruesome twosome. Brilliant! A trophy to show the lads at the club!

Phil and Rod went back to the club that lunchtime with their trophy, Rod's sister Julia tagging along as she fancied a drink. At the club behind the bar was held the clubs' collection of trophies. Since they never won anything sporting these consisted of policemen's helmets, traffic cones, and other things that recorded rather sad moments of personal triumph. While Julia was at the bar getting the round in Phil and Rod told the lads of their particular achievement, embellishing it as one does, and then produced the shoes to the general amazement and admiration of everyone there. The shoes were then passed around to the accompaniment of lots of mature comments such as 'Whaheyyy' and 'Cooorrrrr' etc. The crowd then started to get very loud and boisterous and began an ear-splitting rendition of one of their amazingly witty and original songs about things that most of them had neither seen nor experienced. They swept Rod and Phil across to the bar where to thunderous applause the shoes were handed to the barman who placed them on the shelf of honour beside the four wheel nuts removed from the visiting team's Transit. Cries of 'Speech! Speech!' followed, and gradually the noise died down. it was at this point that Rod's sister piped up for all to hear in her rather plummy voice, 'Rod, what are you doing with Mummy's shoes?'

A second of stunned silence was followed by everyone in the room, apart from Rod, Phil and Julia, falling about laughing. Mustering as much dignity as possible Rod quietly took the shoes back from the barman and without a word of explanation walked out.

Yours ashamed for even knowing them,
Keith.

Dear Father Simon,

I need to confess a sin in order to purge my guilty conscience.

During our summer holidays we were fortunate to be in Devon during the tour of the Radio One Roadshow. Our three children naturally saw the roadshow day as the highlight of our week away.

After the show, most of which I slept through in a deckchair (sorry), the DJ and his two assistants ran across the grass to an autograph booth. I must say I was very impressed by their professionalism and obvious empathy with their fans as they furiously wrote on postcard after postcard.

Radio One is very popular, and, presumably to curtail an autograph queue that would never end, one of the crew got a youngster to hold a pole that read 'end of queue'. Unfortunately one of my daughters was behind the pole. I generously offered to hold the pole for the young lad and, for my sins, moved it right to the back of the queue.

I felt sorry for all the others joining the queue behind me so I moved backwards to allow all of the latecomers to get an autograph, including a young lad who told me he had been round twice so that he could sell them to his school friends! Because the pole kept moving back people kept joining the queue.

Eventually the crewman said something to the effect of, 'Oh dear – the pole's gone,' and the queue did come to an end. I beg forgiveness for making the DJ work much longer hours than normal and I hope his writer's cramp has healed. I cannot remember his name or that of his helpers but we had a great time in Torquay and the children treasure their autographs.

Yours sincerely,
Ray.

Dear Father Simon and devoted congregation,

My tale goes back eleven years, when I was living with my dad and the woman he left my mum for – the wicked stepmother whom I'll call Diane. We only got on occasionally; being only a few years older than me, she was an arch-rival for Dad's attention. During the better times, she used to love to get somebody to wash and style her hair.

One day she decided she would like to try some henna colouring on her beautiful auburn hair, and it was whilst I was out purchasing this for her that I hatched my plan to seek some well-earned revenge.

Before I gave her the pot of henna I added a very convincing 2 in front of the 5 minutes stated on the jar, for time to leave on the hair.

I duly handed over the jar and she asked if I would give her a hand the following week when she had more time. I could hardly wait!

Armed with tin foil and a clock we set about the task of adding a slight tint(!) to her hair. We read the instructions together, piled on the henna, wrapped her head in tin foil and she set the timer. During these proceedings I kept finding excuses for my sudden outbursts of giggles.

Time up, 25 minutes later, off came the tin foil and up to the bathroom Diane went to rinse the henna out.

Unable to control myself any more, I collapsed onto the settee in hysterics and when I heard the banshee-type screams from upstairs, I was certain I'd be found out as my laughing increased dramatically in decibels. I pulled myself together to await the vision, which was by now on its way down the stairs. And then she appeared – Diane in tears with bright orange hair. She re-read the bottle to make sure she had done it right and I managed to convince her that it was probably her hair type that had reacted to the henna and she shouldn't use it again!

Simon, I don't want forgiveness for causing Diane acute embarrass-ment and being the subject of much laughter, by ending up looking like a ripe carrot for weeks, but I would like absolution from all the people with whom she worked for having to look at her wearing a woolly hat during the height of summer!

Yours hopefully,
Hennanonymous.

Dear Father Simon and entourage,

This confession is on behalf of my husband whom we shall call Mike.

In the summer of this year my vandal of a husband, my teenage son and I (note that it is my husband who is the vandal and NOT my son), all went to help my niece move into her house. On arrival there we were joined by three or four of her friends who had also decided to help.

The morning wore on and we were in varying stages of starvation when one dear young man offered to go to the local fish and chip shop to obtain some nourishment. The orders varied from straight fish and chips to curries, peas and beans, etc. – it was a bumper order.

We were all ravenous but not ravenous enough to eat the diabolical food which appeared. My husband, normally a quiet respectable 45-year-old, completely lost his cool as his digestion is very dear to him, and food is a wonderful experience. Without further ado, he picked up the still-full containers declaring that he would have a showdown with the proprietor. He shot out of the house ranting and raving, obviously a force to be reckoned with! He returned later with rather a smug expression on his face. Apparently the shop had closed and in a fit of pique he had posted the lot through the letter box saying they had received their just deserts.

Well, Simon, if this was not bad enough, we visited my niece a couple of weeks ago and were chatting and laughing about her uncle's behaviour when it transpired that he had gone to the WRONG fish shop. In his haste he had not checked which fish shop the young man had gone to. Yes, Simon, this normally mild-mannered man had flipped and posted the food in the shop he thought had tried to poison him. To make matters worse, he knew this months ago and in his shame and embarrassment decided to keep it to himself.

Please forgive him, Father Simon, and give him total absolution or I am sure he will never live it down. Who says vandals are usually the young? Sorry to the wronged 'Chippie' in Barnsley who must have arrived on the Monday morning to goodness knows what. Mike has had many sleepless nights since then and only your forgiveness can help.

Yours sincerely,
A long-suffering wife.

Stratford upon Avon

Dear Father Simon, Sister Di, and Brother Rod,

I feel that it's about time I unburdened myself and sought forgiveness from you. Back in the early 1970s, Crystal Palace were enjoying their very first ever period in what was then the First Division of the Football League. As an avid supporter, both then and even now, I was inclined to attend more than the occasional match. I lived a short five minutes walk from Selhurst Park and being quite unaccustomed to large crowds at football matches having previously only experienced the Second Division or the even lower echelons of the football heirarchy, I took it upon myself to call round in my car to see some friends just before the game. I thought that, even with all parking spaces in the road taken up by football fans' cars, I had allowed myself plenty of time to get home, park the car in the garage at the end of the back alleyway and still make the kick-off.

This particular Saturday, however, Palace were playing Manchester United with awesome names such as Charlton, Best, Law and Kidd in the team. I completely underestimated the extra crowds and how long it would take to get back home and with precious little time to spare I shot into the alleyway to park my car in the garage. I was therefore more than a little irritated when parked just in front of my garage was a car, which certainly did not belong to anyone in my family. Knowing that no self-respecting Palace fan would do such a selfish thing I assumed the car to be one belonging to a Manchester United follower. The 'Follow the Red Devils' sticker in the back window was in fact a bit of a giveaway!

I suppose, with the benefit of hindsight, the owner of the said vehicle did exercise a modicum of common sense since he left the driver's door open, presumably to allow the car to be moved should anyone, like myself, want to gain access to their garages.

However I was annoyed and becoming agitated that kick-off time was approaching, and since the car was owned by a Manchester United supporter, I decided to teach him a lesson.

Aided and abetted by my brother, we carefully pushed the car into the double garage, parked my car beside it, shut and locked the garage door and went to the match.

As usual Palace lost the game, I think it was 3–5 to United, anyway it gave us an opportunity to get back home early and watch the fun when the owner returned to his car after joining in their victory celebrations.

We crept down the garden and into the garage through the rear door and peered furtively out of the cracks around the door to watch the fun. Duly, some minutes later the owner and his friend turned up. There was much pacing up and down, furrowed brows and concerned looks on the faces of both of them mainly because they thought the police had taken their car away. And, when a neighbour, who knew nothing of our little joke, turned up, we could hear him offer use of his telephone to call the police.

When they all disappeared into the neighbour's house we decided that perhaps we should restore the car to its rightful owner, even if he was a United fan. Up went the garage door, out went the car to its original position, down went the garage door again and again we peered out from any available orifices.

It was some time before we heard movement from the neighbour's garden, and voices saying 'I parked it here officer just before the game, there was nowhere else to park anywhere near the ground' when the conversation came to an abrupt halt. The look on the faces of the two Man U supporters and the policeman was a picture.

We decided to make ourselves scarce. We never did find out what the outcome was but the car, the occupants and the policeman were all gone by the time we ventured down the garden later that evening.

We have all moved away from the Selhurst vicinity now so we don't have to suffer football parking problems anymore, but I beg forgiveness for frightening and embarrassing the two Man U supporters, for inconveniencing my former neighbour who to this day doesn't know the truth and from South Norwood Police for wasting their time. With the series of defeats Palace have had at the hands of Manchester United since then, culminating in the Cup Final fiasco in 1990, I firmly believe they have got their revenge albeit unknowingly.

Yours sincerely,
Robin.

Dear Father Simon,

The time has come for me to reveal to the world the events of a balmy summers afternoon which have, to this day, been known only to the two practical jokers involved and the practical jokee.

The jokee, Ian (better known as Chunky), decided that the next addition to his record collection would be Depeche Mode's 'I Just Can't Get Enough.' He duly recruited my friend Gary and me to accompany him to a local record department to make the necessary purchase.

The record was purchased and Chunky was particularly happy with the glossy picture sleeve. He readily agreed to go back to my house for a coffee and to play his new record. When in the house Chunky set about putting on the kettle while I went into the living room to play the new single. However, I hatched a cunning plan.

I switched the record for a copy of Baccara's 'Yes Sir, I Can Boogie' and went back into the kitchen and confronted Chunky with my astonishing discovery. Gary immediately clicked on to what was happening and helpfully suggested that it might be just an error on the record labelling and could be worth some money! Chunky ran into the living room and excitedly put the record on to the deck in anticipation of a tidy packet for what must be a rare record. No such luck.

The opening strains of 'Yes Sir, I Can Boogie' sent him into something of a temper and he was placated only by the return of my mother from work. While Chunky related his unfortunate story to my mother, I switched the records back and, as you would expect from good friends, we offered to be witnesses in the shop so that Chunky could get his money back or a replacement record.

We marched back to the town centre, subtly winding Chunky up into something of a frenzy in anticipation of his forthcoming battle with the sales assistant.

There was quite a queue at the record counter, but undeterred, Chunky strode to the front of the queue, heroically supported by Gary and me on either shoulder, and demanded immediate service as he had been ripped off.

He started blurting out the story to the extremely startled and completely confounded sales assistant and triumphantly withdrew the record saying: 'and when I got it home and took it out of the sleeve it was . . . "I just can't get enough".'

In his excitement, Chunky had not seen his two friends slink away and hide behind the TV theme section of the music department and so, looking around in acute embarrassment, blushed so deeply that two old ladies tried to post letters into his astonished mouth.

He fled the shop pursued by Gary and myself leaving all of the staff and remaining customers in the shop absolutely agog.

We only saw Chunky periodically after that and since the closure of Lewis's in Birmingham and hence the loss of his job as a security officer we have been unable to get in touch for quite a while.

Whilst I suspect that we have blown any chance of forgiveness from Dianne (we upset the female shop assistant in the record department) we would like absolution for these high jinks and if granted could you please ask Chunky to get in touch with me (I think he is living in Moseley) and I will buy him a beer.

Yours sincerely,
Ian.

Dear Simon, Dianne and Rod,

Almost a year ago I made a minor blunder. Being an avid Radio I listener, I decided to nag a few friends into going to the Radio I Roadshow in Bangor.

My partner and I decided to ask our friends if they would like to stay over at our flat so that we could make an early start to the Roadshow, to which they agreed. Early on the morning, at about 6 am to be exact, I woke to the sound of Radio I on my alarm clock radio.

I got up, got ready and kindly made breakfast for what felt like the hungry five thousand but was in fact for just five of us. At about 7 am we were ready to hit the road, and considering the unreasonable hour of day we were all in good spirits. At around 10 am we reached Bangor, having listened to the radio all the way on our merry little journey. Castle Square was the venue for the highlight of our journey, so we were desperately looking out for the Square but to no avail. We stopped our car and asked two or three local folk if they could direct us to our all-important destination, but, they couldn't oblige. At the point of almost sheer desperation, I spotted a local bobby. 'Stop!' I shouted. 'Ask him, he's bound to know.' So we pulled alongside Mr Plod and politely asked for directions to the Roadshow.

'Radio I Roadshow?' he said. 'I'm afraid I don't know anything about that. Are you sure it's Bangor, North Wales, and not Bangor, Northern Ireland?'

A deadly silence fell upon us all, the big smiles we wore slowly disappeared. Yes you've guessed it, we were on the wrong side of the Irish Channel!

Since that day I have had to take severe ridicule from my so-called friends and family alike. The most unfortunate thing about the whole experience is I'm embarrassed to admit I'm a Travel Consultant!

Before I end my letter can you please confirm that the August Bank Holiday Roadshow this year is being held at Sutton Park, Sutton Coldfield, in the West Midlands and that there is no other location on earth that is called Sutton Park?

Yours admiringly,
Samantha.

Dear all,

My confession revolves around an event that took place back in the balmy summer days of June last year. My mate John and I share a speedboat, and our summer relaxation is the environmentally vicious sport of water-skiing. Great fun, but as you can appreciate rather expensive, so the usual thing is to invite along some more bodies to enjoy a day out, and contribute to the costs of the day.

On the day in question, the guests were, well, we'll call them Pete and Liz: friends of John from a previous job. I knew them both, but had only met them twice before. Pete and Liz were both vegetarians, and duly arrived at the lake in the regulation 2CV, with the usual 'Nuclear power, no thanks' sticker in three different languages on the boot. More fun ensued when Pete removed his clothes to reveal a pale undernourished body, in desperate need of some protein. The spare wetsuit was not exactly a good fit, and to say he rattled in it would be an understatement. The day went very well, and as the sun set we set off tired and hungry back to John's house where all was ready for a barbecue.

Why is it, that the length of time it takes to light a barbie is directly proportional to how hungry you are? It took ages, which gave us plenty of time to sink a few G+Ts and review the day's activities. Eventually after assistance from a Hot Air Paint Stripper the charcoal was alight and the cooking could begin, which was just as well because we were all feeling quite light-headed after drinking on an empty stomach. I took control of the cooking, and unwrapped the sausages, beefburgers, and steaks that had appeared from John's fridge. Liz then handed me a pack of frozen veggie burgers. She averted her eyes from the cold meat on the plate next to the barbecue, and requested that I keep her food separate during cooking. I said that I would try, and she returned to her carrot juice.

All was going very well on the barbie, the sausages were fizzing away, the steaks were almost finished, and the beefburgers had been turned once and were just doing nicely on the other side. Just then John came over to check on the progress, as it had been about an hour and a half since we had arrived back from the lake, and he was feeling very hungry. 'All looks good to serve in about two minutes,' I said, 'except for Pete and Liz's veggie stuff, still looks a bit pale to me.' 'Blimey, it does,' said John. 'Move them over the flame.' This I did, the flame licked the veggie-burgers for about a minute, I turned them over hoping to see some change in their complexion but they were as pale as Peter's chest. 'We can't have this,' said John. 'We're all hungry.' 'There's not much I can do about it is there?' I replied.

In an instant the same evil thought came into both our minds. I looked at John, John looked at me. 'We couldn't' we said in unison. 'We could!' we agreed.

John stood guard and kept an eye on Pete and Liz. I picked up a sausage with the tongs and held it over the veggie-burgers and pricked it with a fork. The juices flowed, and I duly covered each veggie-burger with a good coating of pork fat. They really started to sizzle, and in a minute or two went a lovely brown colour. 'Food's up!' I shouted, and the now ravenous hordes descended onto the succulent food on offer. Pete and Liz took their two dark golden veggie-burgers, some salad, and started to eat. I eyed John nervously, but we both choked back a laugh when Liz remarked to Pete that they were the best burgers that she had tasted, and she would buy some more next week!

Julian.

Dear Simon and All,

This tale happened approximately five years ago when I was the tender age of twenty. It was a Sunday evening and a few friends and I were enjoying a quiet drink after a game of cricket. Several quiet drinks later, on the way home, my 'friends' decided it would be a real wheeze to strip me naked and run off with my clothes.

So, there I was, standing in the centre of town, totally in the buff (apart from my socks and trainers) feeling dejected. I decided the only course of action was to go and seek my 'friends' to try and retrieve my clothes. It was now approximately 10.45 pm and as I was walking along the pavement I had a strange feeling that I was being followed! Turning round imagine my dismay to see a patrol car, from which a beckoning finger was pointed in my direction.

Reaching the police car, a grim voice snarled, 'Get in the back.' Not wanting to cause any more of a scene, I obliged the officer and climbed in. 'What's the story then?' he asked. I then told my sad tale elaborating ever so slightly and dropping my 'friends' right in it! After listening patiently, the officers offered me a lift home!

By this time I was feeling very pleased with myself and sat back to enjoy the ride home. (By the way, this was the first time I had *ever* been in a police car.) On the way out of the town a call came over the radio and it went something like this:-

'All units in the vicinity of Smithfield Road, please keep a look out for a yellow Ford Escort which has just been reported stolen.'

By now our car was waiting at the traffic lights at the junction of Smithfield Road and as I casually glanced out of the window I noticed three rather anxious-looking youths in a yellow Ford Escort! So, wishing to repay these kind policemen, I felt it my duty to point this out to them.

'Is that the one?' I said. Suddenly the yellow Ford Escort screeched away, jumping the red light, we followed in hot pursuit.

So, there I was, totally naked, in the back of a police car which was giving chase to a stolen car. With sirens blaring and blue lights flashing, we eventually stopped their car and the officers got out and ran towards the yellow Escort.

After much arguing and shouting, the one officer handcuffed the driver of the stolen vehicle and put him in the passenger seat of the patrol car. The other officer climbed into the driver's seat and said to me, 'Right then, where do you live?' I told him my home address and after a few inquisitive looks from the front seat passenger we arrived at my house.

Unfortunately for me, at exactly the same time as Mr and Mrs Smith, our O.A.P. next door neighbours who had just returned from their bowling club.

'Right then, out you get, and don't let me catch you at this sort of thing again.' I tried to explain to him that my next door neighbours would probably suffer heart attacks if they saw me in my present state, however, my pleas were in vain. 'Out!' he said, so saying my gooodbyes to the kind officer and by now even more inquisitive criminal, I opened the car door and boldly strode down the drive.

'Evening,' I said to Mr and Mrs Smith as they looked at me in total disbelief. 'Evening Kevin,' came the faint reply from Mr Smith who obviously sympathized with my predicament.

Realizing that my keys had vanished with my clothes, I rang the doorbell and prayed it would be answered by my older (and far more sensible) brother. My prayers were answered and I managed to get upstairs to bed without my parents realizing what had happened.

I don't seek forgiveness from the three youths who stole the car, nor from the two kind policemen.

I do, however, seek forgiveness from good old Mr and Mrs Smith, who never breathed a word to my parents about the incident. They have since moved away, but I will never forget the looks on their faces and I'm sure they won't forget mine!!

Yours hopefully,
Kevin.

Bless us Father Simon, for we have sinned . . .

Having lived with in-laws for some months, my husband, myself and our new sprog were delighted to have found a small flat to rent.

Peace and quiet at last . . . or so we had expected. Unfortunately, we soon discovered that our neighbours above were all-night ravers who particularly enjoyed the Sex Pistols.

Night after night we lay awake, young sprog screaming in time to the beat of the ceiling – almost forcing us to contemplate returning to the parents!

Now, pleasures in life were few in those days. Money was scarce and so 'getting away from it all' was out of the question. So, in a thoughtful moment, I planned a romantic and quiet meal for two; rented a movie and invested in a magnum of Johnson's Baby Oil!!

However, I was still only seventeen and had not yet mastered the art of cookery. While the sausages, beans and chips simmered away on the stove, young mother moved to the bedroom to care for her colicky sprog.

Some time later, my husband noticed the smoke curling from the kitchen. He ran to the scene to find the chip pan on fire! Without a second thought, he threw the pan out of the open kitchen window and into the back garden, where it exploded in a ball of flames!

Somewhat shocked and distressed by the event and feeling that life was, indeed, hopeless, we settled down to the movie with tea and toast.

Now, the usual evening entertainment normally started around 10.00 pm so we plugged our ears, doped the sprog and headed to bed. Nothing . . . not a sound . . . we waited and we waited, but nothing happened.

Sleeping to 11.00 am the next day, we felt refreshed and rejuvenated . . . yet somewhat suspicious. The quiet carried on for several days, until we could stand the suspense no longer and called upon our neighbours to find out whether there had been a fatality, or the like.

It was then that we discovered how they had 'got them some faith', 'seen the light' and had enrolled with the local Baptists!

Delighted to hear the news, my first reaction was to ask how such a wondrous enlightenment had taken effect.

Apparently, they had been having tea in their kitchen and discussing Christianity, when suddenly, their net curtains burst into flames! An omen! A sign! At that point, they decided to dedicate their life to prayer and renounce their past.

Father Simon, we now ask forgiveness . . . for the net curtains, for the quiet deceit, for sending such cretins to the Baptists and for singes sustained to a cat passing through our garden on the fateful night!

We hope their faith has acquired a more solid footing. For the sake of our sprog, now 14 and still a light sleeper, we trust in your judgement as a fellow parent in need of a kip!

Aly & John.

Dear Father Confessor and Crew,

When I was small, my family and I lived in a small shack-like house made of fibreglass and wood. My father restored old aircraft and made his living as a pilot.

My story starts early one summer's morning when an aircraft he had restored – his pride and joy – was being towed back to our town by his other pride and joy – his 1962 yellow Jaguar – by his best friend. While on the road, a rather large gust of wind blew his plane off the back of the trailer it was on, and into a nearby field where it completely disintegrated. The trailer jack-knifed into the side of the Jaguar, which swerved across the road and into a ditch – from where it was laid to rest in the local scrapyard.

Meanwhile, back at our little shack, my uncle was giving his girlfriend driving lessons. She had been learning to drive in an old Ford which, when you had finished turning the corner, corrected itself when you let go of the steering wheel. However, she was now in a Land-Rover - which isn't quite the same. She turned the corner round the outside of our house, let go of the steering wheel expecting it to correct itself, and drove merrily on through the side of our little house, straight through the hall, into the kitchen, and finally halted halfway through the kitchen wall, entangled in the plumbing.

My dad hurriedly turned the water off by the stopcock under what was left of the sink – namely a stainless steel bowl attached to a wooden beam that was still standing, and my uncle put down the plastic sink bowl to catch the water dripping from the other pipes.

As the company stood staring in total disbelief at the Land-Rover lodged in one wall, and the hole that had been the first wall (which had totally disappeared, and bits of lagging were beginning to fall out of the roof), my father's friend arrived in a police car to tell him what had happened to his car and plane. This was all too much for my mother, who had lapsed into hysterical fits of laughter, so everyone went into the lounge to try to calm her.

ENTER ME!

Not taking much heed of the fact that our house now only had two and a half walls, and was being kept up by a Land-Rover, I was amusing myself by playing with my doll Vicki. I had decided to give her a bath. Having ascertained that the bowl in which I wanted to bathe her was in the middle of the floor and full of water, I decided to empty the bowl to give Vicki fresh water to bathe in.

I was far too small to reach the sink normally, but thought that if I stood in the hole in the wall behind the sink, with my feet on the stopcock of the mains water pipe, then I could pour the water away in the sink. This I duly did, but as the sink no longer had any downpipe, the water ran straight out the bottom and onto my little feet making them very wet and slippery. In consequently slipped off the stopcock with a scream.

My gallant big brother, hearing my cry, came running to my rescue, only to find that my little feet had rotated the stopcock, the water pressure had built up in the mains, and gallons of water had burst forth into the house in a huge jet, and was rapidly flooding it.

My little form could be seen behind the jet of water, scooting off into the distance as fast as my little legs would go.

My parents, hearing the commotion, came into the kitchen, and seeing what was before them, fell to walloping my poor innocent brother – not believing it was I who had done the dirty deed as I was far too small. Naturally after everything they had suffered that day, they took it out rather vehemently on my unlucky brother.

I would like to confess my guilt to my parents and apologize for aiding in the final destruction of all their worldly possessions; to say how heartily sorry I am for being so callous as to only be interested in playing with my doll whilst their world was falling apart in front of their eyes, and finally for my unpardonable behaviour towards my unfortunate brother in letting him take all the blame.

I am most truly sorry – can I be forgiven?

Susan.

7

Not Quite the National Curriculum

What finer training ground is there for the junior confessee than school? Teachers (particularly student teachers, particularly *French* student teachers), assembly, music lessons, geography field-trips and the bike sheds – an awesomely level playing field. Which reminds me – sports day confessions, anyone? Did anyone ever complete the egg and spoon race/obstacle race/ dressing up race, *without* cheating?

Dear Father Simon and the Holy Order,

The offence dates back to my final year at school; many, many years ago now. The victim selected by myself and my partner in crime, Malcolm, was one John Waring – whom everyone called Theodolite. Now Theo was a trusting soul, a lad with the heart of an ox, but sadly with an intellect to match. Father Simon, I would like to say that Theo was a cruel and vicious boy who truly deserved the punishment we inflicted and that we only acted from the purest of motives. Unfortunately, though, he was an innocent, entirely undeserving of his fate and no motive purer than malice drove us. The opportunity was there and, though I now blush to admit it, we felt compelled to seize the moment.

It had been clear for some time that Theo, for some reason, had the raging hots for my elder sister, Anne. Anne recently had started a course in Swedish massage at night school and Theo's toes positively tingled at the thought of her practising on him. You can imagine his delight, therefore, when one day I informed him that Anne did indeed need to practise for her elementary exams and would he like to join myself and Malcolm as guinea pigs? He, of course, jumped at the chance and the next day saw the three of us, stripped to our swimming trunks, laid out on the patio in the sun, awaiting our massages. Both Malcolm's massage and my own were understandably brief, clearly no more than a warm-up for her pièce de résistance – Theo. His massage went on for over three quarters of an hour, with plentiful applications of massage oil to aid relaxation. Theo was in paradise! Unfortunately, what we had neglected to tell him was that for him a royal blue dye had accidentally been added to the massage oil. The result was magnificent: Arthur of the Britons in his finest woad could not have looked more fiercesomely Celtic. His colouring was truly spectacular. Sadly, though, Theo didn't see it that way and grabbing a towel (for his clothes had by this time mysteriously disappeared) he ran howling back down the road to his home.

From that day on, Theo never spoke to us again. He has since, I understand, found some solace as a Chartered Accountant.

Father I do not plead forgiveness from yourself, nor from Dianne, whose kind heart and goodly nature I know could never refuse a sinner in torment. It is only Rod, stern in his Presbyterian judgement, that I fear might not grant me the absolution I crave – and possibly the studio management collective as well. Only they can free me from my prison of remorse.

Your humble penitent,
Robert.

Dear Simon and the Breakfast Crew,

I have a confession, which dates all the way back to when I was five years old! Do you remember, Simon, the games we used to play at kindergarten? Games such as 'It' or 'Cops and Robbers' or 'Stick in the Mud'?

One such game which was a favourite in our school was 'Choo-choo train'. To begin with, a line of about three or four people, with the dinner lady in front, would all put their hands on the person in front's waist. We would then putter about the playground making 'choo-choo train' noises. This would usually go on until the end of playtime, during which time the train gradually gained length. At the end of break the 'choo-choo train' might be as long as about thirty or so little five-year-olds.

The story begins one playtime, when nothing seemed to be happening. I was very bored and I approached a dinner lady on duty in the playground. 'Let's start a choo-choo train!' I said eagerly. 'Good idea!' she said, and a little two-person train started choo-chooing around the playground. It wasn't long before I felt someone else grab hold of my waist, and felt the presence of someone else grab the waist of the boy behind me.

Now, that's where I thought it would end: a choo-choo train of only four or so people, even though the whole place was echoing with choo-choo noises. So, you can imagine my surprise, when a little later I decided to turn my head to see who was behind me. A line of about fifty or so people greeted my eyes. A mega choo-choo train! At that time I was very shy, and the thought of being at the front of a train that large completely put me out. I did the only thing which came to mind: step out of the line.

I am truly sorry to say that it was not only the boy who was behind me who fell flat on his face, but all the other fifty or so youngsters who made up this 'choo-choo train' also found themselves being toppled to the ground with a tremendous amount of G-Force, and speed.

I was mortified, but not half as much as the dinner lady who had originally led this train; she still to this day thinks it was all her own fault for going too fast in the first place.

Yours,
Michael.

Dear Simon, Di and Rod,

During the early seventies I attended a local mixed Grammar School and it is here that the tale unfolds. One very wet and windy afternoon our double games lesson was transferred indoors (basically because the teachers were wimps) and the class was divided in two. This was because there were about sixty of us and we wouldn't all fit in the gym.

My half was seconded to the main hall to play table tennis on two ancient tables; one on the stage and one on the floor of the hall.

It was during the inevitable wait for a game that I noticed a large, obviously new, black fire extinguisher fixed to the wall in one of the stage wings. It was the CO_2 type, you know, the ones with the big nozzle to aim the gas.

Having a ping pong ball in hand I absent-mindedly wondered if the ball would fit into the nozzle (as you do). It did.

I then discoveed that I couldn't retrieve it, and indeed my efforts to do so only succeeded in jamming it further down. I decided to abandon the scene completely for fear of ridicule from the teacher and quietly rejoined the queue for a game. As you can imagine it wasn't long before I had forgotten the incident completely.

Two weeks later. 8.45 am Assembly.

Centre Stage: large metal box flanked by Headmaster and a fireman in full firefighting kit, complete with large black fire extinguisher.

The Head explained that because the school had been fitted out with new extinguishers, there would now be a demonstration of their use and application by a member of the Devon Fire Brigade. Everyone was fascinated, including me, although mine was due to impending doom more than anything else.

The fireman then produced a large container of methylated spirits, most of which he emptied onto rags in the metal box. He then tossed in a lighted match and stood back with the Headmaster to wait for the fire to reach a suitable height.

What happened next was like something out of a Tom Sharpe novel. After about three attempts to start the extinguisher, the fireman and the Head were visibly worried about the growing inferno, which was threatening to require more firemen than planned. Alarmed, the fireman shook the extinguisher vigorously and yanked the trigger. This was too much for my ping pong ball which with Exocet-like speed and accuracy, shot out of the noozzle, ricocheted off the wooden floor of the stage and hit the Headmaster straight in the 'meat and two veg'!

All hell broke loose. The Head was understandably poleaxed by this unexpected assault and had to be helped from the stage by two colleagues who themselves looked rather apoplectic, either from anger, or more probably suppressed laughter. This took place amidst clouds of smoke, flame and CO_2 as the fireman eventually got around to putting out the fire. The other three hundred occupants of the hall were laughing uncontrollably, all, that is, except me, as I was contemplating suicide, or at the very least, joining the Foreign Legion.

It took ten minutes to restore order, although everyone present was prone to fits of giggling for a lot longer. I escaped detection, although everyone at the table tennis class was interrogated. It wasn't until over a year later that I owned up to my friends, after the Head had retired.

I therefore seek forgiveness not from the Head, who was a turkey anyway or from the other pupils who thoroughly enjoyed the event, but from the poor fireman, who must have thought he was in a living nightmare.

Yours in hope,
Anon.

Dear Father Simon, Mother Di and Little Rod,

I have decided to come clean! My naughty deed dates back three years to when I was a monitor at school in the sixth form. I went to a school in Hereford which is situated right next to the Cathedral (surprisingly enough the school's name has cathedral and Hereford in it!). As it was a religious school each day all 600+ pupils after morning registration were frogmarched into the Cathedral for a service. Chapel as it was called lasted half an hour, during which time a hymn was mumbled, a few prayers were said and a daily sermon was preached.

Anyhow if you were a school monitor (a highly regarded position) as a special treat you had to be in the cathedral by 8.30 ready to enforce the school law and order on the younger pupils – laws such as no talking, eating, coughing and sometimes if they really annoyed you no breathing!

On the day in question, feeling a little lazy I positioned myself next to one of the old tombs with the intention of sitting on it. Now this tomb was one where a statue of the resident lay above the actual tomb. You know the ones I mean, where they are lying on their backs praying.

Well as I sat back, I extended my arm to ensure the most comfortable position possible was achieved. However my palm connected with the stone nose of the resident's statue and to my horror/shock/amazement the nose just slid off. I turned round and picked his nose . . . up. What was I to do? Suddenly going hot and sweaty I popped the 300-year-old nose in my pocket and carried on my duties as normal.

Later on in the day feeling very guilty I popped back and stuck his nose back. But this is the very naughty bit: I stuck it back on with sticky chewing gum, yes straight out of my mouth.

I seek forgiveness for giving this poor Bishop a nose job (well it was a change, he had had the old one for 300 years).

Yours faithfully,
Helen.

Dear Simon, Rod, & 'Miss Dianne',

After many years of deep shame, I feel compelled to confess a dreadful crime which I committed as a youth some twenty years ago against a purveyor of knowledge in my local learning establishment. It took place in the United States, but my guilt is so strong that I can no longer turn away.

I was twelve years old, and living in a very small Midwestern town. Although I was a decent student, the bane of my life (and of the entire school for that matter) was a teacher named Mr Pearce. He was a dreadful man, about a trillion years old, stone deaf, half blind, and in the throes of advanced madness. He regularly marked students down for not attending classes when they were actually there – he just couldn't see or hear them. His grading system worked purely on the principle that whoever could be the biggest bootlicker got the best grades. On one occasion Mr Pearce gave the entire class (myself included) an assignment to complete, an essay on American Government in the 1800s, and the class duly turned in the assignment one week later. The next day we were shoocked to learn that he had failed all of us, saying that we had all written about the wrong subject! He claimed that the assignment was on the Spanish-American War. This was too much to take – we protested to the school authorities. How could thirty-four

people all be wrong and just one (Mr Pearce) be right? Our protests were to be in vain, however, as they knew what a nasty man Mr Pearce was, and tackling him over the issue was more than their jobs were worth. All of us then had to explain to our parents why we had failed – needless to say they found the explanations hard to believe and we suffered various forms of purgatory. I vowed then and there that ultimate vengeance would be mine.

It was about this time that an advertisement was appearing on television for the Volkswagen Beetle. Since Mr Pearce drove one, I had grown to hate them (and still do for that matter). In the commercial, a man demonstrated how well assembled they were by driving one onto a lake, and showing that it floated. I would have dearly loved to have done this with Mr Pearce's car, but I was too short to even reach the pedals, and there was no way that I was going to steal a car anyway. And that's when it dawned on me – if Volkswagen Beetles were so well assembled that they floated because they wouldn't let water lean in . . .

That night I went round to his house with my trusty screwdriver and forced the window of Mr Pearce's Beetle down a few inches. Working quickly, I grabbed the garden hose from in front of his house, placed the nozzle through the window and turned on the water full blast. Thirty nervous minutes later the deed was done – the car completely filled with water, frame resting on the ground. And it worked! It didn't leak out at all either! I decided to complete the effect – I ran home, took two of my pet goldfish from their tank, ran back and put them through the window and into the car. It was clear that they loved their huge new home, and it was a remarkable sight to behold.

The next day at school was one I will never forget. Late morning, the entire school was called into the assembly hall for an announcement. Mr Pearce was in hospital! Overnight, someone had filled his car with water, and when he attempted to evacuate the water by opening the door, he was knocked down by a Beetle-size wave, hit his head on the pavement and had been knocked unconscious! I felt sick – but when they said he should recover in a few days, this changed to total satisfaction. This event proved to be the final straw in his teaching career – Mr Pearce never came back, taking retirement on ground of nervous exhaustion. This might well have been influenced by the fact that the incident was extensively covered in the local newspaper (front page, no less) under the headline 'Teacher's Teutonic Tidal Wave Terror'.

I don't want Mr Pearce's forgiveness, as the old misery richly deserved his soaking, but seek absolution from goldfish lovers everywhere for bringing the lives of two scaly surfers to a premature if somewhat spectacular end. Forgiven?

Fishing for forgiveness,
Awash With Regrets.

P.S. Although his car was fixed (eventually), he was on a water meter and ended up paying for the hundreds of gallons used in the process. Am I still forgiven?

Dear Father Mayo,

I'm writing to confess a dastardly deed that occurred some thirteen years ago. It all started with my father being a rather avid fossil collector. The family were often spirited off to weird and wonderful places in the world – like mid Wales – to look for fossils. My father had a very impressive collection of bits of dinosaurs in rocks. Big deal, I thought, but they were obviously good to my dear daddy.

Anyway, when I heard of a fossil day coming up at lower school, I eagerly begged dad to lend me all his best fossils, so I might take them in and show off. As you can guess he said no, and rather bluntly!

What could I do? The day of the big event was drawing rapidly near, and I still had no fossils. All my pleading to Father was in vain. I was stuck, until my little brain hit upon the idea of theft. Yes, I would pinch a heap of fossils on the morning of the event, hope Daddy didn't notice, and replace them before he came home that evening. Perfect. What could possibly go wrong?

The morning of the day came, and I arose early. I crept downstairs to the fossil cabinet, and stood debating on what to take. I didn't want to take so much that it was obvious I'd pinched some, but I wanted to take something spectacular. I actually took a Plesiosaurus's (or something like that) tooth. This dino's muncher was my dad's pride and joy.

When I arrived at school, brandishing a dinosaur's tooth, as opposed to all the other kids' shells and stuff, I got a wonderful reception. I was the centre of attention, for a whole twenty minutes, before a teacher took the tooth to put it on display. As you can imagine, I was fairly concerned about the tooth, and I made the teacher promise faithfully that no harm would come to it. So I was left toothless in the playground, wondering if I'd done the right thing. I was disturbed by the noise from a small crowd of kids behind me. The centre of attraction was now a small brightly coloured bouncy ball belonging to a fellow playmate named Craig. The ball was fantastic, it would bounce for ever, once hurled at the ground. I soon forgot about my tooth, and by the time we heard the bell for lessons, I had decided that I wanted a bouncy ball more than anything. I approached Craig during number counting (as maths was called in them days!), and asked if he'd swap it for my pencil case? No. My sandwiches? No. My Dairylea slice? Still no. Hang on, what about my tooth? 'Oh, I suppose so,' was the reply from Craig. I waited until break, then ran to the hall where the display was. Sneaking my way past the teachers, I managed to retrieve my tooth without being spotted. I ran back to Craig, and the goods exchanged hands. I was then quite content for the rest of the day – until I remembered my father. Oh dear! I thought, though not using those exact words. I excused myself from my lesson, saying I 'needed to go' very urgently, and ran off in a desperate attempt to find Craig. I was duly informed by a teacher that Craig had gone home sick at lunchtime.

The teacher, obviously sensing that I was fairly distressed, enquired what was wrong. I told her that Craig had my tooth, but I failed to mention the fact that we had a bargain involving a rubber ball. The teacher assumed that Craig had pinched the tooth and done a runner. She assured me that he would be dealt with very severely when he returned to school. In the meantime I was to go home and tell my parents what had happened. So I went home as usual, and told my father the unlikely tale. I was told, very sternly, to retrieve the tooth by the end of the week or I was in deep trouble.

The next day Craig was back at school, and only too happy to swap back, as he was bored with the tooth. Five minutes later, Craig was spotted, and dragged off to the headmaster's office, protesting his innocence. As far as I was concerned Craig deserved what he got for swapping in the first place.

Now I had the tooth back I could relax a little, and was soon involved in a game of tag, and not long later, as happened in all my games of tag, I went down in a heap with four or five others. I was wrestling away happily on the floor, for a full five minutes, before I remembered the tooth in my trouser pocker. Ooops! I stood up, and gingerly removed four pieces of a tooth that had survived intact for 50 million years.

I realize that I did wrong, and believe that I have been punished enough, with the breaking of the tooth alone. I am seeking forgiveness from Rod especially, as he is a man of the world, and is of a forgiving nature.

Yours confessingly,
Andrew.

Dear Breakfast Crew,

At the age of nine, the whole class was involved in a project about India. We studied the Himalayas, read about the Indian cultures, looked at the coins and talked about the history of India. Being the only Asian in the class my teacher would sometimes ask me if I could relate to anything that she was teaching.

She would ask me millions of questions about India and each time I replied that as I came from Bangladesh (totally different country with different religion, currency, language, history, etc.), I knew very little about India. As the poor dear couldn't see past my Asian skin she would persist in asking me about India. These questions did not bother me and I soon realized that if I gave her a half-baked answer with a couple of foreign words thrown in, then she would praise and even thank me for sharing my knowledge with the class. She would tell the class that, 'learning from people who have experienced India first hand was better than any knowledge read from a text-book'.

Being only nine at the time, I loved the attention lavished on me in front of the whole class. I loved the extra questions that my schoolmates asked me about India and I loved playing along with their little games.

One day I suggested to my teacher that wouldn't it be a good idea if I performed an Indian song and dance in front of the class to let them hear the kinds of songs Indian children sing. My teacher wholeheartedly and enthusiastically agreed with me.

The only problem was that I didn't know any Indian dances or songs, I didn't even know any Bengali ones either. The day arrived for my Indian cabaret act. I put on a traditional Bengali outfit (kind of skirt and top with rich embroidery) and tied on a pair of ankle bells and proceeded with my song and dance.

From what I can remember, my song, roughly translated from Bengali, was:-

'I don't know what I'm singing.
You don't know what I'm singing.

It could be wah hah nee nah or shee wah hie and perhaps foaheebah, but who cares.'

So my song went on. I sang gibberish words with an off-key tune and I twirled around the classroom moving my arms; I made everything up as I went along – Clive Anderson would have been proud of me!

When I had finished, everybody gave me a rapturous applause and my teacher said that it was marvellous, and I drank-in all the praise readily. At that moment my headmistress walked in and asked why and for whom all the applause. My teacher enthused about how well I sang and danced for her and asked my headmistress if she would like to see a repeat performance.

My headmistress said that she would love a repeat performance. She also shocked me by saying that she knew a lot about India because she had some Indian friends. 'That's that', I said to myself. 'She'll know I'm a fraud. After all, she did have Indian friends and she was a headmistress, trained to spot fibbing children a mile away!'

But with my head held high and with a deep breath, I repeated my performance as best as I could. The song was even more gibberish, the tune was even more off-key and my dance movements were utterly unco-ordinated.

With my dance over I looked at my headmistress. Her face was blank and expressionless. She stood quiet and still. I watched her heavily lipsticked lips as she broke into a wide smile and told me that I was great. More praise and more applause and from *the head* – I was thrilled!

But now I must say sorry to everyone I innocently misled and conned into thinking that I was performing a piece of classical Indian song and dance when it was just a load of rubbish.

From a repentant student,
Asha.

8

'And We Pay Their Ruddy Grants As Well!!!'

Don't you just love students? Rarely has an appeal for confessions on a specific subject met with such an overwhelming response. Rarely have so few been broadcast. This is because hearing about the miscellaneous urinatory habits of the so-called intelligentsia gets a little tedious after a little while. The following are therefore refreshing in that the toilet does not feature. Much.

Dear Father Simon, Reverend Rod and Deaconess Dianne,

Bless me, for verily I have sinned and caused one of my fellow men to look a right plank. It all goes back to the golden years I spent at Exeter University. In my final year I was living in one of the University's self catering flats with eleven friends and assorted hangers-on. One of our number, whom I shall refer to as Q, was the flat's tame 'wellie' (Exonian slang for Sloane Ranger). He was a likeable chap but somewhat gullible; pull his leg and he'd offer you the other one to pull as well.

One day Q returned to the flat with a tray of coleus plants, liberated from the refuse pile behind the biology labs. For those who don't know, coleus has spearshaped leaves in various colours; mostly red and purple. It looks horrible but the stems are good for budding botanists to cut up and squint at through a microscope. The plants ended up ranged along the window sill in our kitchen, which brightened the place up no end.

A couple of weeks later after a brief foray to the Student's Union bar we were all in the kitchen drinking coffee and putting the world to rights, when the conversation turned to Prince Charles and his alleged habit of talking to plants. Q seemed rather taken with this idea, so we suggested an experiment in which he talked nicely to one of the plants every day, verbally abused another one and left the rest as they were. Q agreed to this and as the days went by he was often to be encountered in the kitchen, telling his leafy friend how it was going to grow up to be big and strong and healthy, or telling the helpless plant at the other end of the row that it would never amount to anything so it might as well drop its leaves and die right now. This led to great merriment and ribald comment but Q continued his experiment undaunted.

Much to everyone's surprise this regime actually seemed to work. The abused plant shrivelled up and died after about two weeks. The other plant rapidly outgrew the rest, and by the end of term had to be put on the floor as it was now too tall to stay on the window sill. Q was delighted and told everyone who would listen about his experiment and its results.

This is where I have to confess that nature had actually been given a helping hand. I was one of the budding botanists mentioned earlier in this letter; and if Q had searched my shelf in the fridge he would have found a little vial marked GA3. As all good biologists know this stands for gibberellic acid which is a plant growth hormone. Unbeknown to Q I'd been sneaking into the kitchen every night and anointing his favourite plant with the aforementioned substance. As for the plant that died; well I dare say it didn't like being watered with washing up liquid.

I should like to take this opportunity to apologize to both plants (the tall one fell over and its stem snapped), to the PhD student whose research got held up for several days because he couldn't find his vial of gibberellic acid, and to Q who was never told what really happened and is probably talking to plants to this day.

Yours in hope of forgiveness,
Chris.

P.S. I know Dianne doesn't forgive animal-centred confessions, but how does she feel about cruelty to plants?

Dear Father Simon, Brother Rod and Sister Di,

After hearing the recent rugby club confession, and your request for student confessions, I feel the time is right to confess my woeful tale.

It all started back in my student days as a keen engineering student at Nottingham Poly. During the first term of every year, the rugby club organized a toga party, which took place about midway through the term.

The party would start in a well known pub near the poly, before going on to a night club on the other side of the city centre.

On the night of the great event, there we all were, wrapped in our bedding consuming large quantities of beer at an alarming rate. As the evening went on, a few of us decided it was time to head off for the night club, and stop for some food on the way.

Walking along the road, we came across every drunk student's dream: roadworks. We could not resist the brightly coloured traffic cones or flashing lights, and soon we were playing rugby in the middle of the road with the aforementioned articles.

After a short time, a very irate man leaned out of an office window across the road and shouted, 'Oi! What the (blank) do you think you're doing?' Without saying a word, one of our party walked up to the front of the building, turned so his back faced the office, then lifted up his toga, as some sort of salute to the irate man. Next thing you know, we were all doing the same thing in a long line down the pavement.

After what can only have been a few seconds, I walked up to the main doors of the office to see who the building belonged to. I returned to the rest of the party who were standing around laughing at the event and calmly told them who owned the building. Yes, you've guessed it! The sign said: Nottingham Constabulary Headquarters'. We then ran off down the road and into the shopping centre, needless to say very quickly.

In lectures the next day, one of the gang was absent. That evening we went round to his house, expecting to find him slightly the worse for wear, caused by the previous night's beer intake. He wasn't there! In fact, nobody had seen him since he had left the night before to go to the party!

We left the house and headed back home. As we walked down the road, we saw in the distance a youth running along the road like he was Linford Christie, wearing nothing but a sheet draped on his body. As he got nearer we recognized him as our missing member.

As he had been walking home from his girlfriend's in the early hours, he had been picked up by the police. It turned out that the irate man that shouted at us was a Chief Inspector, and had interviewed our chum all day trying to track down the unruly individuals who had shown a complete disregard for authority.

I ask for forgiveness not for our party and the fun we had, but because of the interrogation forced upon this lad by the law. Forgiveness from the 'studio collective' would be nice.

Yours repentantly,
Mark.

Dear Simon,

For your listeners' information, Brunel University is a technological university in West London. Its student population consists mainly of electrical engineers, computer scientists, mechanical engineers and a few lawyers thrown in to put a damper on things. Whilst studying in my first year, I met many electrical engineers with an interest in radio broadcasting (I'm a computer scientist, myself).

However, my friends' interest in radio had a slight twist. They built their own radios: Not only that, but they built their own small FM radio transmitters ('bugs' to you, mate). These FM transmitters were extremely powerful, and being at the forefront of technology (as all students are) we were able to build a bug about the size of an old ten pence piece with a range of about 100 metres.

Our halls of residence were split into four floors, and there was always some form of inter-floor rivalry going on. One day, whilst walking up the stairs to my room, I noticed that a member of the floor below me had his door wide open, and it was then that I hatched my evil plan. I dashed into my room, grabbed hold of my 'bug' and legged it back downstairs to the fellow below me. I entered his room and strategically placed the transmitter on the window sill of his room, behind the curtain, and stealthily left, sniggering to myself at the fun I was about to have.

It really did not occur to me that the person living below me had invited his girlfriend down for the weekend. I do apologize for broadcasting his cuddling activities and tonsil hockey to much of Clifton hall.

Worst of all, I apologise for broadcasting on Radio 1's frequency, and for jamming the Bruno & Liz programme. I apologize to all my fellow students who expected to wake with their alarm clock radios playing the latest chart sounds and 1 FM banter, but instead heard a re-creation of heavy breathing and groaning.

Forgive me,
Paul.

Dear Father Mayo,

I sadly have a very true and very shameful confession to make. But before I tell you of the disgraceful behaviour I must first tell you the circumstances in which it was committed.

Seven years ago I was a student studying at Oxford. I had lived in several places of varying squalor, a damp basement flat next to a pub and worst of all, a downstairs room in a shared house with medical students. This particular household would often throw parties on the spur of the moment – without informing me. I would come home from work (a bar job to reduce my overdraft) to find all my furniture in the garage and a great heaving mass of people overspilling onto the pavement. One night whilst at work I overheard a crowd at the bar talking about going on to a party when the pub closed. I remember thinking 'lucky for some!' but thought no more of it. At the end of my shift I returned wearily home, my only consolation the thought of a half-eaten Easter Egg awaiting me, and my bed. The noise hit me as I rounded the corner of my road; sadly I was greeted by one of the aforementioned parties that was already in full swing. The very last straw came when I pushed my way through to the lounge (what was meant to be my bedroom) and found myself pressed up against the very same people I had overheard earlier.

As you have heard the plight of a young student, perhaps you can find it in your hearts to forgive the dastardly deed that ensued. Desperate to move, I began scouring the local papers when I came across a Christian notice board in college. A small advert in a neatly printed hand leapt out at me. Two bedrooms, adjoining kitchen and separate bathroom overlooking a quiet pleasant residential area situated in the north of Oxford. All in all a much sought-after property that was available for a song. It seemed too good to be true. Only £20 a week. However there was a catch. The owners had converted the house and were to live downstairs and let out the rooms above. The couple made it obvious on the phone that they were only interested in renting it out to a fellow believer and regular churchgoing Christian. As I was very poor and desperate to move I knew I just had to get the room no matter what and I was prepared to do anything. I telephoned them again, this time dropping into conversation that I would love to see the property after Bible Study on Sunday – just casual like. Dressed in my leather sandals, I went to meet the couple. I then proceeded to lie and cheat my way into them giving me the flat. I quite surprised myself, I became a different person, quoting the odd parable and telling the owners I attended St Aldate's Church, helped out at the Salvation Army in my spare time and even ran the Sunday School. It was simple. One lie followed another and before too long I had made myself sound like Mother Teresa. Needless to say I got the flat.

But to live a double life was my punishment. Every Sunday morning I had to leave the house early as if to go to church and generally keep up the appearance of a serene nun-like character. I kept it up for five months until it was all too much, but instead of coming clean, I gave my notice to vacate the flat. The charming couple seemed sad to see me leave and asked had I not been happy. I explained to them that I had a vocation and that God had told me to join the Red Cross in Ethiopia when really I had had an offer to move in with my boyfriend. I feel very guilty of conning good people and seek your forgiveness. I still live in Oxford and dread the day when I may bump into them in Sainsbury's. However if it will help my case I must add that for those five months my Mum was happy.

Yours sincerely,
Sarah.

Dear Father Simon, Brother Rod, Sister Dianne etc.,
I am writing to you as I cannot bear the guilt for another day and would like to confess all, ease my guilty conscience and shed light on a matter which to this day continues to bring a furrowed brow and confused expression to the faces of nearly all concerned. In the autumn of 1991, I was a second year degree student in the South West of England, and like my colleagues in the same year, was feeling somewhat miserable at having returned to my studies after the three month summer parole period had ended.

What made things worse was the sight and sound of roughly 200 first year students, or 'Freshers' as they are known in the trade, clearly enjoying the novelty of being at a further education establishment and free of the long arm of parental law. Only Freshers live on the campus itself, and needless to say the college bar was packed every night with this noisy and unruly bunch, racing to spend their grant cheques, latching onto unsuspecting members of the opposite sex and practising their projectile vomiting skills. The bar was practically a No-Go area by the middle of the first week of term to all but Freshers, and the most brave and foolhardy of the remaining students.

On the Thursday night, after my fourth attempt to reach the bar had failed, I sought sanctuary in a cubicle in the gents and sat contemplating which pub I should retreat to, preferably one which might not require unarmed combat experience to get to the bar. Having carefully weighed up the options and made my decision, I chose to depart, but after a three minute wrestling bout with one of the shoe-box-like toilet roll dispensers which had recently been installed throughout the campus, a key fell out of the holder onto the floor at my feet. I examined the key and inserted it in the lock on the dispenser which allowed the lid to be lifted and new toilet rolls to be deposited inside. The key worked! I began to plot my revenge upon the Freshers for keeping me from my beer and forcing me to drink elsewhere at inflated prices!

The following night, Friday, was the night of the annual Freshers Ball, where the first year students do what they do best, i.e. take over the bar and get rip-roaring drunk. *This was an opportunity* not *to be missed!* I had informed a group of friends about me having found the key, and we met outside the bar later that evening. A brief look inside confirmed our suspicions; the beer was already flowing freely, and with an extension to the bar opening hours we were assured that there would be some very unwell Freshers the following day.

'Operation Andrex' began at 20.00 hours. After a nailbiting fifty minutes SAS-style raid, not a single scrap of toilet roll remained! We cleared the halls of residence, refectory, Student's Union, library, teaching and demonstration building toilets (Ladies and Gents), of approximately 250 rolls in total! These were loaded into the car and we fled the scene before being discovered, praying that we would not be stopped by the boys in blue who might enquire as to the contents of the car boot, and spent the evening having an enjoyable drinking session in another bar.

What followed was a weekend of untold discomfort, embarrass-ment, distress and misery for all of the Freshers living on campus, many of whom discovered that most newspapers to not use quality printing ink, that cash machine receipts have more than one use and that sheets of A4 notepaper are not very absorbent! Several swore never to drink ten pints of Irish Stout again without first ensuring that a toilet roll had been locked safely in their room beforehand. Needless to say the

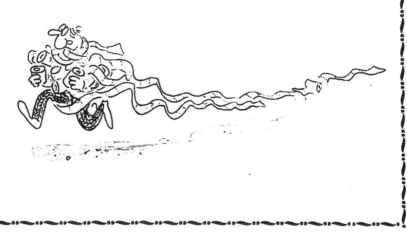

other students thought that this was hilarious, and the whole event was the main topic of conversation for several weeks! I would however like to take this opportunity to apologize. Not to the Freshers, who were taught a worthwhile lesson in what happens when you prevent your academic colleagues from enjoying the college facilities, which are of course there to be shared equally by all, but . . .

Firstly: To the cleaning staff who had to cope with the mess on the following Monday morning, and who had to work overtime re-filling the toilet roll dispensers and clearing the toilets of newspaper blockages, etc.

Secondly: To the then Deputy President of the Students' Union who was blamed for the crime, and who had a very hard time convincing a senior member of the college staff that it was not he who had masterminded the scheme.

And Thirdly: To that same senior member of staff who had a fit when she realized that it would cost over £400 to have all the locks on the dispensers changed to prevent the same thing happening again, had to explain the incident to her supervisors, who never did receive the rolls back as they were re-stolen by an unscrupulous foreign student, and to this very day wonders why her cleaning staff continue to report the theft of toilet rolls from apparently locked dispensers.

I must confess further that I have not purchased a single toilet roll for over two years.

I therefore beg forgiveness, not from Dianne as that would be pointless, but from yourselves and your listeners, adding in my defence that I was sorely provoked, acted in haste and was easily led by my colleagues, and let's face it, we students don't know any better.

Yours repenting unreservedly,
The Phantom Loo-Roll Stealer!

Dear Holy Trinity (and the Collective next door, who we feel are of great importance),

We need desperately to bare our souls to you concerning a wee prank that we played on Herford, a young man with whom we shared a hall of residence in our first year at college. This certain gentleman's motto must have been 'You can dish it out, but you can't take it'.

We digress. Throughout the whole of the first year, Herford played numerous practical jokes on us which included, taking people's doors off their hinges and replacing them with newspaper, tying doorhandles together so that people got trapped in their rooms overnight causing a potential deathtrap, suspending beds above the floor and pathetically blaming it on poltergeists, throwing us fully clothed into cold baths, etc, etc. We could go on, but you'd never be able to fit in, 'On This Day in History'. We took most of this in our stride, and only occasionally sought our revenge. He never took this very well, such as the time when he fell asleep in his room with his door open and we reconstructed his room in the middle of the sports field. If you want to see it we have video proof. Another time we borrowed some of his personal belongings and hid them. When he found them he expected us to apologize for our behaviour. The reply was:

'I'm sorry Herford . . .'

'There's no need to apologize,' he replied frowning.

'No. I was going to say that I was sorry that you haven't got a sense of humour.'

And he still hasn't. You see, we took his jokes in good faith. He however did not take ours very well at all. Time passed and our opportunity for revenge finally arrived.

One year later, we had all moved out of halls. It was the eve of the summer ball and Herford had come to visit. During a break in our hectic work schedule we sat around the kitchen chatting about the year that had passed and our glittering futures. One of us then spied a bottle of vodka, except that it didn't contain vodka. It had been filled with water to be used as a prop in a film that one of us had been making. The only person that didn't know that the bottle only contained water was, yes you've guessed it, Herf. At that moment, we all must have experienced a psychic link, except for, yes right again, Herfy. One of us began to drink the 'vodka' and was quickly joined by another. Some, including Herfy Werfy, declined due to impending assignments. Those of us drinking the 'vodka' pretended to get more and more inebriated and continued to harass Herfy Baby into trying the demon drink. Eventually he gave in. We poured him some of the 'vodka' into a glass for him only to be asked if we had anything to mix it with. The reply was 'Only water'. So we dutifully put a splash of tap water into his tap water. In typical student fashion we decided to down our drinks in one. At this point we expected the Herf of all Herfords to discover that his vodka and water was in fact a double H_2O. However, after downing our drinks he said nothing. We were all a bit gobsmacked. This turned into complete disbelief when he exclaimed, 'I've got a real burning sensation in my stomach'. The following day he said the same thing and even complained of a slight hangover (bless him).

To this day (we are now in the third year) no one has dared to tell him the truth. We feel that we need absolution although all that he really did was humiliate himself. We also seek forgiveness for Herford for not having a sense of humour.

Yours humbly and most profoundly,
Hydrochondriacs Anonymous.

Forgive me, Father, for I have sinned!

I am a student at Leeds Metropolitan University (AKA Leeds Poly until some bright spark thought it would be a good idea to have two universities within a hundred yards of each other!)

I'm currently working on my PhD in Infomatics – the subject you had the nerve to rubbish on Friday's show.

It is the study of different automatic information systems and jolly useful it is too but like many branches of science it has a darker side if placed in the hands of the unscrupulous or vengeful (i.e. yours truly).

My particular area of research is that of inter-relational tele-communications systems – or as we scientists call it 'the phone' and for the past few months I've been perfecting a device for multi-number dialling. Hooked up to any phone, this incredible piece of kit would dial an almost unlimited amount of numbers at once for the cost of a single phone call.

Early last Friday morning as I listened to your show I was putting the finishing touches to the device after months of painstaking work. It had been a marathon stint and I can only claim exhaustion and the euphoria of finishing my wonderful machine in my defence for what I did next.

Hearing you read out the chart-beater choices I thought to myself what better opportunity to test out the machine. The trouble was, how could I be sure it had worked – there was only one tune that was so awful that it wouldn't ordinarily get any votes . . . Yes you've guessed it - the 'Poing' song!

In a fit of excitement I programmed in the number and sent a thousand votes down the line. It was only when I put down the receiver that I was overcome with remorse at the horrible fate I had condemned us all to, but it was too late!

I know I've done a terrible thing but can you and the Crew find it in your hearts to forgive a moment's weakness – after all anybody who has inflicted 'Donald where's Your Trousers' and 'Kinky Boots' on the nation is in no position to be too self-righteous!

Yours repentantly,
Brian.

9

A Nation of Animal Lovers?

Welcome to the largest collection of stories in the book. Animal abuse is of course not funny, but sometimes – even with the very best of intentions – accidents happen. I, like you, love all tropical fish, locusts, cats, dogs, horses, cows, foxes, goldfish, mice, flies and snails (particularly on toast with lots of butter), but I still forced a reluctant titter at the following catalogue of calamities. And be of good cheer – my vicar says all animals go to heaven. Perhaps I'll try the other place.

Dear Father Simon, Brother Rod and Sister Dianne,

Having heard your request this morning for animal confessions I have decided that now is the time to seek absolution for not one, but two grievous sins concerning animals from my dark and distant past. Both occurred about twelve years ago, and I leave it up to you which, if either, you choose.

The first concerns a goldfish by the name of Rudolph. He was the pride and joy of my friend, Jane, who saw fit, for reasons known only unto her, to entrust Rudolph to me while she departed for two weeks' holiday with her family. Rudolph was thus safely installed on our kitchen worktop and at first everything went swimmingly. We had been warned, however, that Rudolph fancied himself as goldfishes' answer to Houdini and was prone to jumping out of his bowl for no apparent reason. We therefore devised a mesh of chicken wire to place over the top of the bowl to prevent Rudolph from practising this potentially fatal hobby. One day, however, things did not go to plan. Being mid-summer, I was wandering around the house in bare feet and went in to the kitchen to grab a snack. When I stood on something slippery and a bit mushy, I simply thought it was a bit of mashed potato, dropped by my mum in her haste to feed her hungry offspring. On closer inspection, it turned out to be Rudolph. Yes, I had stood on my friend's goldfish. Well, you don't expect to find a goldfish on the floor, do you? My scream brought my mum running and fortunately she had the presence of mind to scoop poor Rudolph up and slip him back in his bowl – he hadn't been completely squashed and was flapping about feebly. I was a quivering wreck in the corner and couldn't even look at the results of my footwork. Rudolph survived for a couple of days on a diet of neat brandy – we weren't sure whether his lop-sided swimming was as a result of his accident or the alcohol. Unfortunately, he finally slipped away to the great fishbowl in the sky where he could perform his acrobatic feats in complete safety. When Jane returned from holiday, I told her a censored version of the sad tale – how poor Rudolph had leapt from his bowl, and was not discovered until it was too late. I didn't see the point in upsetting her further with the true sordid story of how I had stood on him.

My second confession also concerns my clodhopping feet. My sister and I had a small colony of gerbils, which we used to exercise by letting them run loose along the corridor of our bungalow, having first shut all the doors. Someone would be appointed to sit with them to keep an eye on them, and at first we performed this task together, spending hours devising new combinations of toilet-roll tubes for the gerbils to run through/chew up. After a while, however, the novelty of the task wore off and we would take it in turns to sit in the corridor with a good book while the gerbils cavorted around us. On the day in question, it was my turn to gerbil-sit. Unfortunately, it clashed with my tap-dancing practice. I decided that, if I used the tiled floor in the bathroom for my practice and left the door onto the corridor open, then the two activities could be combined. This worked well until Stevie-gerbil (named after Steve Ovett before we discovered that he was a she when she produced four babies) decided to investigate the rhythmic tapping emanating from the bathroom. Her entry unfortunately coincided with a particularly complicated time step. There was a rather sickening crunch and my heart stopped, not to mention the time step. Not daring to look down, I leapt out of the bathroom in a single bound and sat shaking in the corridor. I couldn't bring myself to look at the bottom of my tap shoe for fear of what I might see (visions of the more violent scenes of Tom & Jerry flashed in front of me). Eventually I yelled to my mum, who came to my rescue. On closer inspection, the bottom of my tap shoe yielded no signs of the accident, but Stevie-gerbil was definitely a goner. Funnily enough, I gave up tap dancing shortly after that.

I don't expect Dianne to grant forgiveness for either of the above (although they were both accidents), but I hope that you, Simon, and Rod can find it in your hearts to forgive me and relieve me of the terrible burden that I have carried around for so long.

Yours sincerely,
A sinner in Sevenoaks.

Dear Father Simon,
I am writing to ask your forgiveness for a little incident that happpened when I was but a mere lad, twelve to be exact.

The scene: a boarding school in the New Forest. It was an old building and the science labs were housed in what would have been the coach house and stables. In the biology department there were several pickled animals, skins, skulls; the usual stuff. But in the summer term we used to have a couple of cages of locusts.

I remember my parents driving me to school for the first day of the summer term. We would always stop off at Beaulieu Aerodrome, a disused Second World War air strip. We would sit and watch other children playing with their remote-control planes; I was really envious of their toys.

Anyway, back at school: The first few days would be spent as normal, swapping stories of what happened during the holidays; what films we'd seen etc., etc. After a week, boredom had set in and I wandered around to find some mischievous activity.

I know . . . the biology lab has got its new batch of locusts, I thought. So off I went to sit and gaze at these ugly creatures. I then had a brainwave. Thinking back to the airfield and the remote-controlled planes, I went up to the matron's room, dug around and found some cotton thread. I rushed back to the biology lab and grabbed an unsuspecting locust who was sunning himself under an electric light bulb. I carefully tied the cotton to his back leg, made sure nobody important was around and walked out into the courtyard. Holding on to the end of the cotton thread I carefully opened my hand. The locust walked to the end of my finger and set off for its maiden voyage of freedom. I watched for about five minutes as it flew in circles around my head. I truly felt proud of my new sport; not only was I having fun but I honestly believed the locust was enjoying this new lease of life. Being at a boarding school myself, I could relate to the locust held prisoner in his cage. This was going to be my new hobby for the summer term!

The next occasion was a beautiful sunny summer's day. My chum the locust and I were safely in the courtyard ready for another flight. Cotton thread attached, the locust took to the air. Once again there was great excitement as the locust flew round in a circle above my head. Suddenly there was a 'swoosh' and the cotton thread lay limp on the ground at my feet. All that remained of my mate was a twitching back leg.

Above me a house martin returned to its nest under the roof overhanging the courtyard.

At first I was devastated. Then I thought of a new sport: Falconry! (Or rather, House Martinry.) I dashed back into the biology lab to get another locust, harnessed it up and returned to the courtyard for my new game. The locust took flight and sure enough, within a few minutes a house martin swooped down. This was miles better than any radio-controlled plane, this was true sport. I decided that I would have to ration myself, otherwise the biology teacher would get suspicious of the reduced locust population. I decided that once a week I would take just one locust, from a different cage each time. This continued for the whole of the summer term.

I don't ask forgiveness for the original sin of remote-control locust flying. I think both locust and I got quite a thrill out of the adventure. But could you find it in your hearts to pardon a young scientifically inquisitive child who was always on the look-out for new ideas?

Gavin.

Dear Simon,

You've heard of Smokey and the Bandit, haven't you? Well, my confession is called Smokey and the Tunnel.

Smokey was my friend Brian's beautiful and arrogant grey cat. The tunnel was a heavy wooden one through which Brian's Hornby train would run. On rainy afternoons we would play with it, but Smokey was not welcome to join us, as he had so many times before pounced on the train as it sped past him, causing the most awful crashes.

On this particular day, Mallard was pulling all of the eleven trucks that Brian possessed, when in strolled Smokey. Knowing Smokey's past form for creating railway disasters, I brought the train to a halt, so that Brian could remove his marauding moggie.

To save the guard from a severe headache under Smokey's paws, I pulled the train just inside the tunnel. Smokey tensed, his eyes opened wide and he snuck forward, his chin on the deck, until his nose was just inside the tunnel mouth. I made the train move a little more, and as the brake van disappeared into the gloomy depths of the tunnel, Smokey tried to follow it, until the whole of his noble head filled the opening and his sleek stomach was laid upon the Up Main Line. Then I made the train crawl off slowly to see if he would try to struggle after it. Smokey, however, remained unmoved, still staring into the inky blackness, oblivious of the fact that all of the train was now out of the tunnel and moving slowly down the back straight.

Brian and I looked at each other, our minds working as one, but MY hand was on the controller.

I spun it round until it was hard against the stop, and all twelve of Mr Hornby's very best volts galvanized Mallard into action. Wheels spinning, scrabbling for grip like Nigel Mansell launching his Williams Renault from pole position, she hurled her heavy train around the long bend, and when she reached the straight leading to the tunnel, her connecting rods a blur, she was the perfect reincarnation of the REAL Mallard pounding down Stoke Bank to take the World Speed Record for Britain all those years ago.

Doubtless remembering all the times Smokey had abused her in the past, I swear that she was still gaining speed when she struck that wicked pussie's posterior, and as she did so, several things seemed to happen at once.

Mallard stopped, very suddenly, the rest of her train crashing in a heap around her, and the red button on the controller went 'plop'. Not 'plip' or 'plup', but 'plop'.

More startling by far was the effect on Smokey. Nothing in his evil life so far had prepared him for being unexpectedly walloped in his posterior parts by a fast and heavy express train. Not only did he let out a banshee wail that echoed through the tunnel, but he also shot about a foot and a half straight upwards. I swear he'd have nearly made the ceiling, but he was hampered by several pounds of tunnel around his neck, which of course went up in the air with him.

A moment later, through our helpless tears of laughter, we could just glimpse a grey furry streak bolt for the bedroom door. Smokey never EVER came to play trains with us again.

Simon, I crave your forgiveness after all these years, not for giving Smokey his comeuppance, which of course he richly deserved, but for misusing such a magnificent model locomotive.

Am I forgiven?

Chris.

Dear Simon, Rod and gorgeous Di,

I am currently a PhD student studying cell biology at Cambridge University, but when I was younger I had aspirations to become a veterinary surgeon. I was told that in order to obtain a place at a veterinary college, I had to have a considerable amount of experience of work in a veterinary practice, and it was during one of the periods I spent in various veterinary practices that the following events occurred.

It was getting towards the end of the regular morning surgery when a young, rather shy couple, with a reluctant golden retriever in tow, entered the examination room. The vet greeted the owners and asked what was wrong with the dog. The husband replied in a quiet, timid voice that the dog was 'having trouble with his motions'. The dog was gently lifted onto the examination table and after a brief investigation the vet confirmed that the dog was indeed constipated. At this point I should say that this was not a serious complaint and could be easily cured.

The vet reached into a cupboard and retrieved five oval-shaped tablets that were about two inches long and three-quarters of an inch wide. The vet told the couple that these large tablets were required due to the size of the dog. He placed the tablets in a small envelope and wrote the dosage instructions on the outside. Then with the words 'these are for his back-passage', he handed the tablets to the couple, who by this time were looking extremely flushed. The couple paid their bill and left the surgery.

The rest of the examinations that morning occurred without incident, and we swiftly moved into the operating theatre, to get through the regular catalogue of castrations, etc. The vet had just begun operating when the phone rang; it was the husband in a rather distressed state. Apparently, they had misunderstood the vet when he said 'these are for his back passage', and had taken this to mean that the tablets were canine suppositories. As you can imagine the poor dog was in a state of considerable discomfort and could apparently be heard some distance down their street.

Upon hearing this the vet literally collapsed on the floor in a fit of hysterical laughter. When he eventually recovered his breath he clarified that the tablet was actually supposed to be crushed and given to the dog by mixing it with a very small amount of dog food.

I do not seek forgiveness for myself but I would like to appeal on behalf of the young couple, who are probably desperate to write themselves, but are still too shy. Additionally, I think it is about time someone apologized to the poor dog, who probably had 'trouble with his motions' for a long while after the constipation had been cured!

Yours sincerely,
Martin.

Dear Father Mayo,

As a keen horsewoman one of the main activities of the summer was to compete in as many shows as possible. After an especially disappointing season when I was twelve . . . well, OK, fourteen actually, I decided at one such show that I would get my own back on a fellow competitor who had gloated over my horse, Bumbles and I, with her winnings all season.

It was a fairly big show and I was just putting the final touches to my horse when *she* strode past looking immaculate and all ready for her first class which was 'Best turned out horse and rider'. She was always sickly-sweet towards me which meant you could never be nasty to her. Anyway she stood watching me for a moment and seeing I was in my usual panic, asked if she could help at all. In that second the evil plan flashed through my mind and the Devil within started tittering. 'Actually', I said, 'you could pick her feet out for me' (a cleaning method – for all non-horsey people). 'How about tying her up over there on the straw which has been scattered about?' Amanda readily agreed. Puffing out her little chest with self-importance she did as she was asked. Now Bumbles has a habit of lifting his tail and expelling – shall we say – solid matter soon after he is led on to clean straw. Only in summer, when the grass is rich, it is not quite so solid (and very green).

I busied myself putting away bits and pieces into the horse box whilst watching from the corner of my eye. Bumbles performed right on cue, whilst Amanda was bent double, peering down and cleaning with gusto, Bumbles' hind right leg. The shriek that she emitted caused a chain of events that upset more people than you can imagine. A class going on nearby took fright and two ponies backed into and sat on a jump, another horse broke free from where he was tied up and caused havoc, dispersing a crowd within a few seconds!! And someone else dropped a tray of drinks. however the best sight of all was Amanda. She hadn't sprung away from Bumbles quick enough and most of *it* was in her hair, some was smeared on her blouse but a lot of it was on her whiter-than-white jodhpurs. Meanwhile, I had slumped against the horse box having absolute hysterics – I can honestly say I have never

157

seen anything quite so funny before or since. I know it was a bit mean but I beg forgiveness not only from Amanda but all the people whose day I messed up at the show, especially from the bloke who probably spent a tenner getting the drinks only to drop them all. I would very much like forgiveness from Dianne, as I'm sure she knows how cut-throat these horsey events can be.

Very hopefully yours,
Andrea Owen.

Dear Father Simon and the crew,
I seek forgiveness for a misdemeanour which occurred way back in January 1992. A few friends and I had gone into town to indulge in our hobby of drinking pubs dry, and we returned home a little worse for wear to say the least.

As always happens at that time of night we started to get a little peckish and stopped off at my friend Mike's house to order a delivery of pizza. It is here where my wicked deed occurred. (I should point out that Mike's parents had gone out for a meal and left him in charge of the house and its contents.)

Whilst Mike was upstairs searching around his trouser pockets to find some money to pay for our order, I became extremely impatient and had a rummage around in the pantry desperate to find some morsel which would stave off my pangs of hunger. It was after Xmas and the pantry was very well stocked with left over mince pies, Xmas cake, chocolate biscuits and other goodies.

My eye landed on a huge tub of toffee popcorn and with an excited whoop, I tore off the plastic lid and began shoving great handfuls into my mouth like a man possessed. As I walked into the living room, my friends were equally pleased to see this big tub of grub and they too began to dig in.

It was then I noticed the rather sad and hungry faces of the tropical fish which glided around inside a large illuminated tank beside the TV. Poor old things, I thought. Swimming around all day with nothing to do but eat a few flakes of fish powder and bash your head repeatedly against the sides of the glass.

So in a flash of inspiration, to a mixed display of both bemusement and horror from my friends, I lifted the lid of the tank and began to sprinkle large quantities of the Toffee Popcorn along the surface of the water.

And I must say the fish absolutely loved it. The whole lot seemed to disappear in a matter of seconds.

I hurriedly replaced the lid as Mike returned to muffled laughter and a few red faces. No one said a word.

The pizza arrived, and as I live in a public house I suggested we head off there for a further bout of drinking to wash down the Pepperoni, Chilli with extra Chilli, and Mexican Hot we had ordered. All in all it was a good evening which lasted into the small hours.

I spent most of 1992 living and working in London, and although Mike and I stayed in touch it was only during a recent chat that I casually enquired how his father's pride and joy, his fish, were getting along. 'Fine,' he said. 'Although we did have a bit of trouble with them just after Xmas. They got very bloated one day and a lot of them died off, I found them on their backs floating along the surface. My dad thinks it was some sort of disease, some of the smaller fish looked to have warts on the insides of their body. They were enormous.'

It was only then did I realize what I had done, I had singlehandedly wiped out an entire colony of fish with my offer of some Yuletide popcorn. The fish had quite literally stuffed themselves to death. To this very day Mike and his fish-loving family are completely oblivious to my drunken act of Fishslaughter.

Yours sincerely,
David.

Dear Father Simon, Brother Rod and Sister Dianne,

Seventeen years ago, when I was the tender age of four, ten minutes of innocent play has resulted in my conscience being darkened ever since.

At the time, we lived on a dairy farm on the outskirts of Carlisle, and with no brothers or sisters then, very often there was very little to do, apart from watching the greatest team on earth, Carlisle United, every Saturday afternoon.

One summer's day, bored with my sand-pit, Tiny Tears and Tonka Trucks, I ventured into a field to play with the cows. The cows drank from an old cast iron bath in the middle of the field, although at the time I believed it was where they had their daily dip. Having watched my mum wallow in a deep Radox bath, wouldn't it be lovely, I thought, if the cows could have a luxurious bubble bath too? I was sure my mum wouldn't appreciate me using her bubble bath for the cows, so I decided to search in the farm sheds for some. Success! A lovely container of green bubble bath, marked with red lettering. I carried it back over the field to the bath and poured the liquid in, mixing it carefully with a stick.

My bubble bath was forgotten about until several days later, when a convoy of vets, police cars and local newspaper reporters arrived at our farm. Apparently, my 'bubble bath' was a container of concentrated weedkiller, and had resulted in the death of one cow and the severe illness of three others. The police suspected two local characters who had recently been released on bail on charges of arson at another farm, resulting in these men being brought in to the station for questioning, but later being released. My parents and I had our photo taken for the local rag, with me holding the empty container of 'bubble bath' – I think the cutting is somewhere in our attic.

I now wish to seek forgiveness for my actions seventeen years ago – forgiveness from my parents for their financial loss and disturbed state of mind (permanent), from by the police for their wasted time, from the two men who were questioned by the police, and forgiveness from you. You should know that I am now a respectable law student, totally against animal cruelty and a member of Greenpeace.

Anxiously awaiting your decision,
Erica.

Dear Sacerdotal Simon and the Confessional Crew,

Whoops! I'd better confess for I have taxidermally transgressed. Two years ago my next door neighbour decided that she needed a break from her secretarial job in Ipswich and booked a ten-day holiday in Belgium. Before she left she asked me if I would mind keeping an eye on her house, watering her plants, etc. while she was away. I said that I would, so she left me her back door key.

Now, there are two things about this neighbour that you should know – she never misses an episode of Coronation Street, and about a year and a half before this little event took place she began to collect stuffed animals. Up to this point she had bought three, a mallard, a pheasant and a fox – all of them fellers. Although I don't particularly like the thought of storing dead animals in a living room, I had nothing against her little collection, that is, until I saw her peering over the hedge at my cat and two kittens that were snoozing in the sun on the lawn – she had a sort of 'Ooooh, they'd look great on my mantelpiece' type expression on her face. It was at this moment in time that I decided to adjust the woman's attitude towards little living, fluffy creatures.

My chance came while she was on holiday. I entered her house and, after eating a packet of crisps which I found in her pantry, I removed the ex-fox that was running across the top of her television in a state of non-animation. I placed the poor chap in a black bin-liner, tucked him under my arm and took him to my workshop. My workshop is my pride and joy – it is here that I make and mend all kinds of electrical gadgets, remote control vehicles, etc. Indeed, I am a bit of a wizard when it comes to electronics.

In my workshop I set about 'operating' on the fox – a project that took me the best part of two days. After this time I had successfully loosened the joints of the creature and given the tail a certain amount of flexibility. I had also inserted a simple system of small electrical motors which would drive an even simpler lever system into the parts of the fox whose days of cunning were no more. Are you getting the picture?

I returned the fox to its deathly still position of running across the top of the television, plugged it in and set the timeswitch that I had, at considerable expense, purchased for this very cause. It was perfect, the lead and wall socket were hidden behind the telly and the fox, despite my adjustments to its inner self, had not visibly changed. It was Wednesday morning. She, the collector of former furry animals, would be returning that afternoon. Coronation Street would begin at 7:30 that evening, the timeswitch was set for 7.45.

I sat in silence at home, listening to the wall. At precisely 7:45 I heard a scream that would wake the dead, followed by a rather worrying crash. I dashed across to her house to see what had happened. She was sitting in an armchair crying and shaking, the fox had stopped whirring, squirming and twitching, there was a trail of coffee across the carpet, leading from the armchair to the telly and a mug nestled in the television where the screen used to be. In between hysterical sobs she explained that her fox had 'come back to life' and she thought that it was 'going to get her'. I poured her a stiff drink and told her to go to her bedroom and lie down. As she was going upstairs she asked me if I would mind 'getting rid of the animal'. I grinned, told her that I would kill it for good this time and, while she was upstairs, I removed the timeswitch, electrical lead and the star of the show himself. Two weeks later she had sold Mortis the mallard and Frigid the pheasant, and she hasn't bought any taxidermial terrors since.

OK, what's the verdict? Am I forgiven?

P.S. Is it true that old Bates is slowing down in his old age? If you send him to my workshop I could have him rewired and moving again in a couple of days.

Anonymous.

Dear Father, forgive me for I did sin. Quite by accident, but sin I did. Some years ago when I was at the tender age of seven and a half years I liked, as most children of that age, to be as helpful to Mummy as possible, which on many occasions would get me housebound, but that's another confession.

It was a day like any other, I wandered lonely round our three-storey house, which at my age seemed enormous, anyway, in our main lounge which was out of bounds to me, were the usual furnishings – nice sofa, winged chair, lamp tables, piano and 'Pinky and Perky' the goldfish, looking this particular day decidedly dirty. Idea!! . . . I'll clean out the fish! I took the bowl down very carefully, put it on the floor, then shut the door to downstairs, where both my mother and the cats were residing.

I then proceeded upstairs to get my ceramic potty, painted with a daisy, and daily – unbeknown to me – cleaned with bleach, with some left for the sake of hygiene.

I rushed downstairs filled with joy at the prospect of doing something of a great deal of help for my mummy and my sister; she would be pleased as Pinky and Perky were hers, she had won them at the fair. Anyway very gently I proceeded to tip the goldfish into the pot, then wiped the bowl out with my best hankie and of course the hem of my dress, then returned Pinky and Perky safely to their now clean bowl. There was a knock at the front door. It was my friend Sally, and as with most children my mind almost immediately turned to play, so gently Pinky and Perky were returned to their place on the piano, and I could go to play happy in the knowledge that I had been a good girl today.

Sometime later I returned to find that the whole family had congregated in the lounge, my sister had returned from work this evening and as usual first priority would be to feed Pinky and Perky, HORROR!!!!! . . . It would seem according to my mummy that poor Pinky and Perky had gone to heaven, and that the cause of death was a mystery!

Althought I was only seven and a half and angelic, common sense was something that I had in abundance, plus my sister was sixteen and very touchy: if for one moment there was any doubt in her mind that I was even remotely connected with this incident, it would have been death by the most horrible of means available to her.

A very nice service was held in the garden that night. So all that remains is that forgiveness is given all round, I am truly sorry.

There is one more sorry to this and that is to Smokey the cat, who being feline, was as most people know, fond of fish, and unfortunately on this particular occasion, when he dug up poor Pinky or was it Perky? for his supper he wasn't aware of the circumstances surrounding their departure from this world. Don't worry though, Di, he didn't die, he just came that evening and sicked on the carpet.

I know that Di is going to find it difficult to forgive but it was an honest mistake.

Yours very, very sincerely,
Yvonne.

Dear Father Simon,

My sin occurred some twelve or thirteen years ago on a hot summer's day at the beginning of the school holidays. On the particular day in question, my elder brother, Mike, and myself had worked ourselves up into a mischievous frenzy at the looming prospect of two work-free weeks on holiday in sunny Devon. We had finished all our packing and were looking for a way to while away the remaining afternoon.

After growing tired of running the toy soldiers over with the Scalelextric we were drawn downstairs by cries and screams for help coming from our mum. Imagine our delight at finding all the fuss was over the cat; Lenny bringing in a dead mouse as a going away present. Strangely enough Mum didn't feel fit to accept the gift, so as dutiful sons we picked up the dead furry thing, scolded the cat and said we would throw it in the bin immediately. Now of course being young and inquisitive we were not going to throw away a live (or at least recently dead) mouse until we had determined the cause of death in typical Dr Quincy MD fashion. Unfortunately before we had time to scrub up and get stuck into the autopsy mum called us down for dindins, so we packed the patient into a shoe box and put it into the cupboard for later examination. But you know how forgetful twelve and thirteen-year-old kids are and after a thrilling episode of Starsky and Hutch the mouse had completely left our minds and we were much more interested in who was going to scoff the most ice-cream on holiday.

And so the situation remained as we departed for sunny Devon and returned two weeks later a little fatter and a tad more sunburnt. Everything was going swimmingly, we were all in good mood and even Lenny the cat seemed happy to see us, a situation which was soon to change as Mum went up to freshen the rooms, as mums do. Soon after disappearing upstairs the whole house was filled with such a terrifying scream coming from Mum and our bedroom that the whole family ran upstairs to see what was wrong. There, our Mum stood (or rather ran round in excited circles) in front of the open cupboard, covered from head to toe in large, evil looking bluebottles; it was like a scene straight out of 'The Exorcist'. You couldn't even see out of the window for the covering of little black bodies, not that Mike or myself were hanging around to look though, young we may have been, stupid we were not. We realized the flies must have come from the decomposing body of the mouse and also that we would be for the high jump if it was found out who put it there. We knew our only chance was in solidarity and finding some poor sucker to use as a scapegoat. In our case that goat turned out to be furry, miaow a lot and go by the name of Lenny. Quick as a flash and with the agility possessed only by a terrified kid I located the now very smelly skeleton of the mouse and showed it to Dad explaining that the cat must have caught it and hid it in the cupboard just before we went on holiday. Luckily for us the story was accepted and the cat kicked into the back garden with all of us shouting after it what a useless animal it was.

I'm sure in writing this that I speak for Mike as well as myself when I ask for forgiveness; not for all the torment poured onto Lenny over the following weeks nor for the guilt at being the cause of death for so many thousands of flies at the hands of my Dad. But rather I ask for forgiveness for the psychological damage caused to my Mum who must still shudder at the thought of opening a cupboard door for fear of what lurks behind it.

Yours,
Dave.

Father Simon,

I am writing to confess my animal sin. This year I have taken my A levels, and part of my biology course was to carry out an investigation. Mine was to examine food preference in the common snail. I'd just like to say here that the snails were looked after very well and suffered no cruelty. I was supposed to test preference between carrot, lettuce, cabbages and onion but the snails appeared to prefer the Blu-tak holding up the lid of their tank – by the way, do you know that snails' droppings turn blue when they've eaten Blu-tak?! Anyway the snails brought much amusement to our biology group – especially when they escaped and I had to stand on a bench with a fishing net scraping them off the ceiling. Well, when the Christmas hols came, I had to take them home with me. They lived in the dining room, and I cleaned them out everyday. Before I went back to school I decided to soak their tank in hot water to get rid of all the blue droppings. This meant putting the snails somewhere. I put them in a bucket with clingfilm on the top, putting holes in the clingfilm, of course! When I came back with the clean tank, the clingfilm had disappeared, and the snails were all over the dining room. I collected up as many as I could find, but I couldn't remember how many I had originally. The snails went back to school, and the term passed relatively quietly. In the Easter holiday my Mum had a dinner party, with some quite posh people. Half way through the meal, snails quietly slid along the dresser. Everyone was too polite to comment, but my Mum wasn't very happy! The snails must have gone into hibernation, and woken up when the hostess trolley was turned on. Anyway, I'd like to beg forgiveness from my Mum and Dad for ruining their dinner party and I'd like to beg forgiveness from the snails, which appeared to be a bit constipated after eating the clingfilm.

Claire.

10

Peace and Goodwill to All Men

It's Christmas. The loveliest time of the year. A time for sharing, caring and . . . weeing on Santa, killing mice, putting Granny in hospital, stealing the baby Jesus, swearing at Mary and Joseph, and shooting your parents. No wonder it's so much fun!

Dear Father Mayo and the wise men and women in your stable, I seek absolution. The terrible deed happened in the Christmas of '71 when I was only five years old.

Like any boy of five I loved Christmas. The anticipation leading up to Christmas Day was as much fun as Christmas Day itself. Every year my grandmother used to take me and my two brothers for a special Christmas tour of London. To us London was Lapland and the place where Santa Claus lived. We all looked forward to the trip so much that we hardly slept the night before.

Once in London we walked about the streets sampling the dodgy hot chestnuts, gobsmacked by the streets shows in Covent Garden and generally overawed by London doused in lights and splendour. As always the finale was meeting Father Christmas in Selfridges. Grandma always kept this to last. In fact it was the only way she could get us to behave. She used to say, 'Father Christmas will know if you've been naughty today.' On hearing those words our underdeveloped Adam's apples used to quiver and we quickly fell into line.

Before seeing Santa, Nan treated us to a milkshake as the queue was always long and she didn't want us moaning for a drink once in line. Leading up to the grotto we could do nothing else except talk about what we were going to ask Santa for Christmas.

The wait always seemed like eternity, but we didn't care. At last it was my turn next and I was nervous. Nan took me by the hand and led me down the dark plastic cave leading to Santa. There he was, long white beard, leathery skin, clad in red with shiny black boots and the cotton wool in all the right places. He reached out his hand and before I knew it I was sitting on the lap of Father Christmas. WOW!

But the excitement, the anticipation and the milkshake were too much. He asked me what I wanted; it wasn't Action Man with gripping hands or a new 'Chipper' bike - but the loo. It was too late. I had weed on the leg of the real Father Christmas! He quickly stood up holding me outstretched and uttered a few words, the only one of which I understood was 'kid'. There I was, mouth turned downwards quivering at the edges still locked in the sitting position like a parachutist in his harness whilst being held by Santa who didn't know what to do with me. My grandmother wasn't sure whether to spank me, help me or kidnap a fairy's costume and blend in.

I seek forgiveness, firstly to Father Christmas who couldn't change clothes because the line had got longer in the commotion and people were beginning to tut. Secondly to my grandmother who eventually went to my help when she wanted to disown me. Also to my brothers who never managed to see Santa and never forgave me until Christmas morning. And lastly but by no means least, the little girl with a lovely white dress who was next in line.

Carl.

Dear Father Mayo and the Breakfast Crew,
Let me take you back three years to a cold Christmas Eve's night. I had been invited to my girlfriend's parents house for the first time. They were both retired academics who lived in a large, gothic-style detached house, hidden in the suburbs of Cambridge. Arriving there, I crunched up their long, shadowy drive as the wind whistled through the huge trees that surrounded the dark building. I was very nervous to be meeting Alice's parents, but the intimidating sight of this spooky house was making me tremble.

I was immediately put at ease, however, when my knock on the front door was answered by Alice's mother, Edith. She gave me a warm welcome, planted a kiss on my cheek and ushered me into their glowing living room. The room had a heavily laden and colourful Christmas tree with presents scattered underneath it. Alice's father, Albert, was sitting in a leather armchair in front of a roaring log fire. He had a beard and white hair which on that particular day reminded me of a certain jovial red-dressed man who would be delivering presents to the children of the world later that evening.

I joined Albert in front of the fire with a glass of port while the rest of the family prepared the dining table. It was at that point that Snowy made an appearance. Snowy was the family's pet mouse which was allowed to roam freely in the house as they didn't like keeping him in a cage. It was a friendly, home-loving animal, I was told, that had never tried to escape, even though it had many chances to. I remarked how kind it was to treat an animal in such a way, and conversation soon got round to our collective beliefs in vegetarianism.

Albert and I were deep in conversation when dinner was called. While we were talking, Snowy was crawling on my leg but I hadn't noticed that he had settled on the end of my foot. As I uncrossed my leg and stood up to go to the dinner table, I simultaneously heard a crackle and pop from the fire. On uncrossing my leg I had propelled Snowy into the open fire where he came to a crispy and well-done end.

I can't describe what happened afterwards as it is now all an

embarrassed blur. Needless to say dinner didn't last very long. The odour of roast mouse isn't a very appetizing smell.

It is with deep remorse that I ask for pardon, not only for causing the terrible death of Snowy, but also for causing Albert to drop his pipe onto his lap, setting his trousers on fire. I would also like my identity kept secret as I would not like my fellow members of the Anti-vivisection League to know I had caused the cruel death of a poor animal.

Yours sincerely,
S.

Dear Father Mayo,

On behalf of my mother I wish to offload the guilt of a secret held in the family closet since the perfect family Christmas of 1979 when a lively bottle of tonic water nearly brought disaster to the household.

Picture the perfect family Christmas scene with Mother, Father, brother, Gran and Great Gran, 82 years of age and marginally senile, sitting around watching the Queen or anything else served up by the television companies after a thorough stuffing of turkey.

In an attempt to enliven the proceedings, Mother, well known in the family for not quite being the full shilling, offered drinks to the family. For reasons known only to herself, Great Gran requested a whisky and tonic water and duly received a large tumbler containing a triple whisky diluted to the top with tonic water. With dainty 82-year-old elegance this was downed and about twenty minutes later a further tumbler of tonic requested in order that she might take her heart pills.

After taking two tablets with the tumbler of tonic, I noticed with amusement that the old bird was slurring her words slightly. Mild amusement changed to marked interest when she started to slump in her chair. The slump then deepened into a deep, deep sleep. It was only when she failed to be roused by prodding, loud talking, slapping around the face and other strenuous attempts to wake her that we decided something was obviously very wrong. An ambulance was called.

In the short time between the ambulance being dispatched and arriving the cold realization dawned. One week previously, Mother and Father had attended a party. The bringing of a bottle had been requested but being cheap they had bought a bottle of vodka and decanted half into the only available receptacle before proceeding to the party armed with a half full bottle of vodka. Of course, the only available receptacle had been an empty tonic water bottle which had then assumed the identity of a full bottle of rather flat tonic water. Mother had given her gran two full tumblers of vodka only slightly diluted by a triple whisky. The downing of just under half a bottle of vodka in just under half an hour was now obvious as the cause of her slumbers. In addition, she had taken two heart tablets.

The ambulance duly arrived, its aerial bedecked with Christmas tinsel and condoms, the paramedics equally as festive and the drunken biddy wheeled away to hospital to be examined. There were many curtains twitching in the quiet cul-de-sac as the ambulance departed.

At hospital, she was, not unsurprisingly, pronounced very drunk but otherwise OK and the heart pills identified as diuretics. By this time Great Gran was beginning to get a little frisky. Never ever drunk in her life before, the alcohol was having strange effects on her brain's inhibitory centres. Doctors were propositioned and flashed at as they passed this normally quiet and demure 82-year-old lady. Once reasonably sobered, she was sent home to sleep it off and we were sent away.

Expecting a very groggy hung over Granny the following morning Mother was surprised to be woken at 6.30 am Boxing Day by the sound of Gran washing pots with fabric conditioner, completely oblivious to the previous day's events.

Father Mayo, I seek forgiveness for Mother, whose attempt to enlived the usual boring family Christmas resulted in one never to be forgotten. Please forgive her, not for the Granny whose taste buds couldn't tell the difference between tonic water and neat vodka, who didn't even suffer with a hangover and who, to her dying day, never knew why she managed to miss the James Bond film. Father Mayo, I seek forgiveness on behalf of the Mother from the ambulance and hospital staff who had to deal with this mini crisis on Christmas Day and who were quite marvellous and patient. Perhaps a reminder of those who have to work to care for others over the festive season.

Tim.

Dear Father Simon, Sister Dianne and Brother Rod,
Forgive me, for I have sinned. My sin is as follows:

About twelve years ago my local village was thrown into turmoil by the commission of a terrible crime.

Each year at Christmas time a local church erects a Nativity scene in the shopping centre. It is a large wooden structure with figures representing all the primary players in the Nativity including cows, sheep, Wise Men and of course the Baby Jesus. The scene is very lifelike, well as lifelike as is possible with three-foot tall figures made from plaster of Paris, although they do use real straw! To add to its authenticity there is no glass in front of the scene and small children gaze on it with wonder and delight (poetic licence there).

One night approaching Christmas my two friends and I were coming home from a quiet evening spent playing spin the bottle and drinking cider (usual behaviour in this town where there is almost nothing to do and as I am sure Brother Rod could tell you the Devil makes work for idle hands). Our route home took us through the centre of town where the Nativity scene was set up. We stood behind the small fence designed only to keep gnomes and very small children away from the scene, admiring the tranquillity and beauty of it all. Suddenly I was seized by a devilish thought.

Jumping nimbly over the fence we approached the stable (really a three-sided garden shed) and quickly whipped the Baby Jesus out of his manger. My friend stuffed Him down the front of his coat and off we ran into the night.

Oh! the guilt and fear of discovery weighed heavily on us. I wouldn't keep Him at my house for fear of discovery so it fell to Simon to provide temporary accommodation for the little mite. We began to go around with gaunt faces and the worry started keeping me awake at night (I wasn't born to a life of crime!). When the story made the front page of the local paper then we decided it was time to make amends.

Simon brought Baby Jesus to school in his Liverpool Football Club holdall and we planned that we would somehow return Baby Jesus to his rightful place. That lunchtime we hurried to the offices of the local paper. We decided to make it look as if Baby Jesus had made his own way back and that he was seeking shelter at the offices of *The Formby Times*. We sneaked up to the door, placed the Christ Child on the step, rang the bell and ran for it.

The paper reported the re-appearance of the Baby Jesus but instead of, as we had hoped, continuing the mystery, the paper simply described us as 'youths' seen running from the office.

Simon, I would like to beg forgiveness, not only from The Man Himself but also from the people of Formby. From that time onwards the Nativity was screened by a large pane of glass, spoiling the realism of the scene and thus the enjoyment of everyone in the town.

Yours remorsefully,
Carol.

Dear Fr Simon, Rev Rod, Sr Di. & The Holy Order of the SM Team,
After a great deal of soul-searching, anxiety and, above all, guilt, we
have decided it is time to confess to a most heinous misdemeanour
involving vandalism and perversion of the course of justice.

The wicked acts took place at Christmas time in the late '80s at
which time we were a young couple who were leaders of our local
Youth Fellowship group. This group was basically a collection of young
people who met once a week in our local church and did 'church-type'
things interspersed with deeds more normally associated with such a
group of young people (helping old ladies across the road, sweeping
paths in winter, etc.). It was traditional for our group to go out carol-
singing the Sunday before Christmas and this particular year was to be
no exception. The usual practice was to drive a small van around the
streets of our village with a Santa perched on top ringing a large bell.
This served two main purposes – it helped to drown out the dreadful
singing of the 'troops' walking behind the van, and aroused people's
curiosity so they looked out of their windows and could not then turn
out the lights, hide behind the sofa and pretend they weren't at home.

Unfortunately, the van we usually used was not available that year
and we were in danger of losing one of our most essential pieces of
equipment – particularly as our Santa was not the type of person who
enjoyed walking for miles in a ridiculously heavy outfit. Luckily, one of
our happy band had recently started work for a well-known TV rental
firm and he offered the use of his company van. This solved our
problem and the great night soon arrived. The van appeared at the
church at the appointed time and was duly decorated with snowmen,
Christmas trees and other festive images using white spray snow. Santa
was perched on top and off we went, merrily disturbing everyone's
lazy Sunday evening viewing and gratefully accepting large amounts of
cash.

On completing the evening's work, our group dispersed and we
returned home to count the takings which were later forwarded to a
local children's hospital. However, around an hour after finishing, the
telephone rang and a rather distressed TV rental repair man informed

us that he had cleaned down his van but had a problem. Apparently, the spray snow that had earlier decorated the van so cheerfully was not the type of substance you should spray on shiny, metallic paint and that the areas it had covered were now far less shiny and in fact devoid of the paint that had been there previously. To make matters worse, one of our group, after the carol-singing was over, had decided that some of the snowmen should be snow-women (very liberated and modern group that we were!). He had therefore sprayed the appropriate extra anatomical features onto the previously asexual snow-people.

Extremely concerned, and not finding this revelation in the slightest bit funny, we asked him what he thought we could do – bearing in mind that his use of the van for such a purpose was likely to result in the loss of the van and the gain of a P45. He asked if we would mind taking a little trip to the local police station with him to 'assist' in his reporting of the incident for insurance purposes. His report went along the lines of: 'Good evening, Officer. I was at the pictures last night with my two friends here and when we came out my van had been sprayed with fake snow by some local merrymakers. I tried to clean it off today but have found that it has lifted the paint off the van.'

The kind officer took down all the details, including the 'witnesses'' (us) names and addresses and said that the TV company should contact him if the report was required for insurance purposes.

We do not seek forgiveness for the vandalism of the van (we didn't do that anyway!), nor for our acts of prevarication in the police station as this was done purely out of compassion for our innocent and helpful friend who did not deserve to lose his job for performing an act of charity. No, we seek your forgiveness for leading such dreadful singing then, and in other years. In our defence we can only say that we are no longer involved with the group (as we are too old) and that we did raise large amounts of cash for charity.

Yours repentantly,
Mr & Mrs X.

Dear Father Mayo,

I am writing to seek forgiveness for an incident that took place on a cold Christmas Eve some twelve years ago when I was an immature sixteen-year-old, living in Brussels.

The festive season always heralded a string of parties either side of Christmas Day and 1982 was no exception. They were the type of parties when the parents always got incredibly drunk and the children got thoroughly bored.

The party at the Jacksons on Christmas Eve was no exception to the rule – while the parents were getting sozzled upstairs, the children were left in the cellar to play table-tennis, darts or beat up a bloke called Greg who was generally disliked.

The beating up of Greg is not the sin for which I seek forgiveness – no, it is for what happened to a guy called Tony. Let me explain: while in the cellar playing darts, I inadvertently missed the dart board and hit a polystyrene village that was lying on a nearby table. The village had been tirelessly crafted and built by the Jacksons' daughter, Rose, for an A level project that was to be assessed in early January. The pleasure that I got out of seeing the dart go through one of the cottage roofs was wondrous. So, with my next throw, instead of aiming for the dart board, I aimed at the polystyrene village and well, you can guess the rest. The game soon caught on with the other children who abandoned their dull activities to partake in the wholesale destruction of the village. But the mayhem did not stop there – other breakable objects were hunted, located then destroyed – lampshades, light bulbs, train sets: nothing breakable remained in once piece. Bomber Harris would have been proud. Pandemonium ensued for fifteen minutes, all because of my inability to emulate Jocky Wilson.

As the destruction escalated, I suddenly became anxious to leave the party. I persuaded my parents to leave 'the bash' because 'I felt very sick'! My parents fell for my act and I was rushed home to bed.

A few days after the party, the Jacksons came round for dinner and told my parents about the mindless vandalism that they had discovered in their cellar after the party. I again felt very ill but a wave of relief passed over me when the Jacksons announced that the culprit was Tony, who had been spotted by the Jacksons' son, Andrew, examining the former polystyrene village. Tony's protestations that he was completely innocent (which was true) were not accepted. Thereafter, Tony was only allowed to go to Christmas parties if he stayed close to his parents. No wonder he always looked so miserable.

I would therefore like to seek forgiveness from:

1. The Jacksons, for causing a mini-riot in their cellar.
2. Rose who had to build a new polystyrene village for her A level assessment,
3. Tony, for not owning up to my inadvertent instigation and involvement in the mayhem which led to him being labelled a 'problem child' by the parents on the Brussels party-going circuit.

Yours,
Sonia.

Dear Holy Bunch,

You might think that nativity plays are the very epitome of Christmas – children sweet and angelic acting out that first Christmas story, glowing faces, proud parents and warm hearts. Most of this is usually true, but at St James Primary School in 1967 things got slightly out of hand.

In our school it was always the top infants class that got to perform the traditional play. Even though we were young the jostling for the best parts started early. Unsurprisingly the roles of Mary and Joseph were the most sought after, followed by the three kings, then came the shepherds and various assorted angels, cattle and so on. As I had played the part of the Pied Piper in a school assembly three months previously I have to admit that I fancied my chances of getting Joseph or a gold-bearing king at least.

Unfortunately for me and my best mate Darren, we were caught throwing our school potatoes at the class weed who was called Tom. The consequences of this harmless event were calamitous. I neither got the role of Joseph nor a king nor a shepherd but that of third innkeeper. I was truly gutted. Third innkeeper? It didn't even merit a mention in the programme, or duplicated sheet to be precise. How could I impress my fellow nine-year-olds as a pathetic one-line-only innkeeper? For the record my words were as follows: 'Sorry, we've no room.' Hardly going to impress the school was it? To make things worse, the boy who teased my sister for having a big nose got the part of Joseph, and got to rehearsals with the delectable Jennifer Wilkes who was selected to play Mary. All us grown up nine-year-olds fancied her, well as much as a nine-year-old can any way.

Revenge was clearly called for. There were three performances of our nativity play and I decided that it was the last one, on Friday afternoon, with all the parents in dutiful attendance, that was to be the target of my shockingly well planned spite. So the scene was set. The stage as I recall looked a picture – Bethlehem AD 0. The First Christmas. A nervous Mary and frightfully overacting Joseph approach the first inn; towels on heads and tied dressing gowns about them. 'Is there any room at the inn?' intoned Joseph. 'Sorry, we're full,' says *innkeeper 1. On a few steps. 'Is there any room at this inn?' says Joseph again. 'Sorry, we're full tonight,' says innkeeper 2. And on they come to my inn. I've been waiting.*

Now I have to say in my defence that I didn't know the meaning of what I was about to say. It was something I'd heard one of the top years say. I knew it was a naughty word but that was it. Back to the stage. Knock knock. 'Is there any room at the inn, please?' says the dreadful Joseph. And in my best acting voice I said, 'No. Bugger off!'

Looking back I suppose it could have been worse. But not at the time. To say that there was an audible intake of breath is an understatement. To say I got a belting is an understatement. Needless to say this was the end of my acting career and I'm now a supermarket manager who tells his staff off for swearing.

Yours in humble supplication,
Tom.

186

Dear Simon, Mz 'D' and the rest of the crew,
I wish to confess to you all about my Boxing Day prank in 1989.

It concerns my five-year-old son (who is now eight years old and completely recovered from his ordeal), and his grandfather (my dad).

I was separated from my wife and living at home with my parents at the time. My four children were spending Boxing Day with me.

I had bought David (my son) a radio-controlled tank as his present. It was a beaut. 360° turret, with ½ mm gun, machine guns, missiles, three forward and one reverse gears, and video-screen targetting. (Saddam would love a fleet of these.)

We had our lunch and numerous drinks, and we all retired to the lounge to watch the afternoon film. My father slept on the sofa face down.

Bored with the film I decided to give my son's tank a test drive. I sent it round the room, over the dog's ears and knocked over various drinks on my front room 'recce' operation. I realized then that the tank was about five feet from my father at about 90° to the side of his head.

I switched on the video viewfinder, armed the guns, and lowered the main gun turret until I had my father's left ear in my sights. With an evil grin I pressed the 'fire' button. The tank then launched a ½ mm earwax-piercing shell, smack, straight in his lughole. Perfect shot.

My father jerked about two feet off the sofa, still horizontal.

I quickly replaced the handset in my son's hands.

You may guess the rest; my father jumped up, snatched the tank off David shouting and snarling, 'I'm putting this away and you can go and sit upstairs until tea-time!'

David, protesting his innocence, and doing a good job of trying to grass me up, was dragged upstairs kicking and screaming. My Father returned five minutes later saying things like, 'Those tanks are b----- lethal in the hands of children.' I sat and said nothing.

Can you forgive me? My son still tells his grandfather 'It was Daddy.' And am I covered by the Geneva war convention?

Yours faithfully,
Ian.

Endpiece

And so dear brother/sister, it's your turn. I know you have committed many, many lamentable deeds in your life. Now you have the chance to lift the burden not only off your shoulders but off the Mayo overdraft. Feel free to write to me at:

IFM
London
WIN 4DJ

All letters will be dealt with in strictest confidence, and then passed around the office for a good laugh.